SUCCESS CODES

SECRETS TO SUCCESS YOU WEREN'T TAUGHT IN SCHOOL

BRIDGET AILEEN SICSKO   ANOUARE ABDOU

ASHLEY GENE PINKERTON   CARLY FERGUSON

CHANTEL PORTER   DANIELLE MOORE

DIANA POULSEN   DINA BEHRMAN

FRIEDERIKE SADHANA VON BENTEN

JEANNIE MORAVITS SMITH   JESSICA HOEPER

JOCELYN CHONG   KELLY TAN   KRISTI HRIVNAK

LINDSAY RAE D'OTTAVIO   LIZ COALTS

MARIKO BRENNER   NATALIE LOWRY

POONAM MANDALIA   SIOBHÁN PHOENIX

SOFIYA MARIYA   STEPHANIE C KOEHLER

TATIANNA MICHALAK

CONTENTS

Introduction   v

1. Anouare Abdou   1
How authenticity led me to my dream job (and led me to quit it)
   About the Author   11

2. Ashley Gene Pinkerton   12
With the Spark of One, the Flame is Lit
   About the Author   21

3. Carly Ferguson   22
Let Your Truth Be Your Identity
   About the Author   31

4. Chantel Porter   32
Success is Found in the Wild
   About the Author   40

5. Danielle Moore   41
My Light
   About the Author   48

6. Diana Poulsen   49
The Core Elements of Embodied Success
   About the Author   60

7. Dina Behrman   62
The Journey To Inner Success
   About the Author   70

8. Friederike Sadhana Von Benten   71
From Stress to Success: How to Gracefully Master Crises
   About the Author   84

9. Jeannie Moravits Smith   85
Success: It's an inside job. Maximize Your Human Potential
   About the Author   94

10. Jessica Hoeper, MSW/LISW   96
Success is Collective.
    About the Author   106

11. Jocelyn Chong   107
Vastness Of Success
    About the Author   117

12. Kelly Tan   118
You Hold the Power to Define Your Success

About the Author   129

13. Kristi Hrivnak   131
Success Is Being

About the Author   139

14. Lindsay Rae D'Ottavio   140
The Bottom Line Is You Are Exactly As You Are Meant To Be

About the Author   149

15. Liz Coalts   150
Pretty Damn Successful Right Now

About the Author   157

16. Mariko Brenner   158
Success is MAGNETIC: You can't hustle your way into alignment

About the Author   166

17. Natalie Lowry   167
My Road to Success was a Four Act Play

About the Author   176

18. Poonam Mandalia   177
The Lioness Roars

About the Author   181

19. Siobhán Phoenix   182
Success Means Reconnecting With Our Soul As a Part of a Multidimensional Universe

About the Author   190

20. Sofiya Mariya   191
Womb Alchemy: Your Portal of Success

About the Author   198

21. Stephanie C Koehler   199
From Fear to Fierce: Forging Your Own True Path to Becoming Unapologetically YOU

About the Author   208

22. Tatianna Michalak   210
The Harmony of Success

About the Author   218

23. Exalted Publishing House   219

INTRODUCTION

Success to me has always been an interesting topic. I grabbed my first copy of *Think & Grow Rich* in my early twenties, proceeded to devour it, and then annoyingly recommended it to all I encountered.

Sorry friends, I tend to do that with *a lot* of books.

I've always desired money. And for most of my life, as many do, I equated money to success.

I remember growing up watching *MTV Cribs* enamored by what money could afford people, yet confused when the lottery winners in the news went bankrupt.

I was deeply inspired by *HGTV House Hunters* and those with huge budgets, yet confused when wealthy, "successful" celebrities became addicts or took their own lives.

I didn't understand.

I thought success was the answer to everyone's prayers and the be-all end-all, but evidence showed differently.

And it was a pivotal moment in my own life when my own dad, who to me was the epitome of success, had a health crisis of his own.

My personal interest in uncovering what success really is has taken me down a path of looking at my own deeply-held beliefs about money, my family, success, my health and how I'd like to spend my days.

I came to terms with the privilege I grew up with.

How I viewed money.

How I spent money.

How I perceived my own success, and got honest with myself about my unintentional, deeply ingrained, continuous quest for success.

I've learned that success is much more of an internal condition than a material fulfillment.

I've learned that health, family, values, and spirituality cannot be left out of the success equation.

I've learned that it's safe to desire money—and it's safe to make money—but that does not define someone as "successful".

One of the reasons I came up with the concept for this book was because of my own upbringing and thoughts on success.

Growing up, I had a very comfortable life: a beautiful home, loving parents, nice cars. From society's perspective, it was all that is desirable. I had many privileges that I still to this day do not take for granted.

In Sedona a few years ago, my dad, a highly successful entrepreneur, business owner, and singer, began waking up in the middle of the night unable to breathe. It was so scary, scary enough to become a huge puzzle piece in my success redefinition journey. After he drove himself to the ER in the middle of the night without telling *anyone,* I started asking myself some questions.

"Does success even matter if you don't have your health?"

Nope. The answer came quite easily.

Success isn't what they teach in schools.

It's not what is shown on TV or in movies.

It's a lived experience of redefining what it is; and it's quite personal.

In my own success code, I believe my health, family, relationships and values are the core to this code.

It is my deepest desire that in the coming pages of this book, you too can awaken some of your own truths about success.

You may be reminded that success isn't really even about money; it's about something much more.

And most importantly, it's up to you to choose how to live your beautiful, successful life.

-Bridget Aileen Sicsko

1

ANOUARE ABDOU

HOW AUTHENTICITY LED ME TO MY DREAM JOB (AND LED ME TO QUIT IT)

*H*ad I known that setting the intention to live an authentic life would end up being so disruptive, I might have chickened out. But when I made the decision one evening after work, nothing changed on the spot aside from the fact my skin was wrinkled from sitting in the bathtub asking myself existential questions (and finding answers). Why didn't the dream job I had worked so hard for feel fulfilling?

I don't think any of us initially walk around wondering whether the things we value come from soul-level truth or trauma-based response, or whether our self-worth is built on a foundation of external factors such as achievements. The craving for more authenticity is often born out of a lack of integrity—a nagging feeling that becomes more glaring the more you try to ignore it.

I had always been incapable of separating my work from myself, which blessed me with a fast-evolving media career driven by the culmination of my interests and strengths. From reviewing restaurants to interviewing celebrities, I had experienced several "I can't believe I'm getting paid to do this" moments. Lacking authenticity wasn't exactly on my radar.

Becoming the managing editor of a large North American lifestyle publication at the age of 28, only a year after joining the team as a junior editor, was supposed to be "it". So why did it feel like something was off? Like "it" was elusive?

It was not the best question to ask, but it was a starting point that led to more conducive introspection. At first, I turned outwards. Well-meaning friends and respected colleagues told me work wasn't supposed to fulfill so many needs, that there were pros and cons to every job and that switching jobs wouldn't guarantee satisfaction; why risk it when I already had something good? When I turned inwards, I wondered if I was destined for a lifetime of unfulfillment, driven by the pursuit of a goal only to quickly become dissatisfied once it was reached and until the completion of the next goal, and so on, like a dog chasing its tail. I wondered what was wrong with me and why I couldn't simply be grateful for an opportunity many would want—an opportunity that I had wanted badly myself.

I also wondered what was wrong with society. Was this supposed to be adulthood? Was I missing something? Was this "it" forever? I felt uneasy at the thought of my schedule depending on others for years and years to come. Watercooler conversations about Netflix shows bored me.

I daydreamed about vacations even after coming back from one, and started feeling a pit in my stomach on Sunday evenings following weekends gobbled up by a couple of errands or a hangover induced by the urge to blow steam off after a week filled with meetings, deliverables, and office politics. I felt a pang of sadness for a coworker who had been in the same role for fifteen years and seemed to have lost a certain sparkle in his eye. But maybe that was presumptuous. Maybe he was content. Maybe he had priorities I couldn't understand.

However, if I felt a void despite having attained my desired career, and if I was drained despite not managing responsibilities such as parenthood, I concluded the source of my dissatisfaction was either myself, the job or the paradigm for work.

As it turns out, it was a bit of all those things.

From the catalyst for my authenticity journey to its anticlimactic unfolding and from landing my dream job to quitting it, here is a glimpse into what the pursuit of an authentic life has looked like for me. You will also find principles for authentic success to help you navigate your own path.

THE REFLECTION THAT CHANGED EVERYTHING

What happened during my momentous bath was that, instead of trying to figure out what was wrong or what to do next, I took a moment to block out all external noise and connect to my heart's deepest desires. "If what others think, including the people you love, didn't matter, if what you think you *should* want didn't matter, if what looks good on paper or sounds prestigious didn't matter, if the amount of people who would kill to be in your place didn't matter, and if you didn't have to make any compromises, what would you want?" I asked myself.

I wanted to be myself at work and be surrounded by people who inspired me. I didn't want to wear masks or endorse upper management decisions I didn't agree with. I wanted to believe in the mission of my organization and the impact of my work. I wanted to have decision-making power. I wanted the same salary or more, but with deeper meaning. I wanted a leadership role, as I had fallen in love with management and the business side of media even though I had started out as a journalist. I didn't want to sacrifice working for a big publication with millions of readers. I wanted to continue traveling. I wanted Mondays to feel like Fridays. I wanted growth and a constant stream of exciting new challenges and opportunities. I wanted life to feel like a genuine, heartfelt expression of my soul. I wanted authenticity in every breath.

THE INITIAL ANTICLIMACTIC UNFOLDING

The next day, I didn't march into my boss' office and quit my job in a dramatic display of f*ck-it-ness, although viral videos of people doing so were all the rage on social media back then. But I did carry myself with a slightly different energy, a budding sense of relief awakened by the act of dusting off my inner compass. Now that I had set the intention to live an authentic life, I didn't have an immediate solution to my work predicament, but the fog of confusion and resistance was lifting to unveil a glimmer of trust and possibility.

I kept an eye out for job postings but didn't want to settle for anything that didn't feel like a "hell yes". I still experienced some dread and swallowed moments of resentment, but also listened to uplifting content during my daily commute. I wish I could tell you I was authentic 100% of the time from that point on, but that's not how intentions or human nature work. It starts with tuning in and listening. The best we can do is aim to be aware of moments of misalignment and gently steer ourselves back towards what feels more of integrity: decision by decision, action by action, reaction by reaction.

There are thoughts, wants and feelings that genuinely come from within. There are times we make ourselves fit into a neat little box. Sometimes it looks like succumbing to social pressure and knowing we're self-abandoning but not being brave enough to do anything about it. Other times, it's more subtle. Life can feel like wearing a sweater we would like if it wasn't for the slightly itchy fabric, but wear anyway and end up regretting it all day.

Without concrete benchmarks such as knowing when we're people-pleasing versus when we genuinely want to say yes, it's impossible to embody authenticity. It can get complex, nuanced, or straight-up paradoxical, because we're multifaceted beings who live on a planet where contrast allows subjective experience to exist. Without the resistance that led me to observe a lack of integrity, I wouldn't even have known how to translate integrity into action, or define it in the first place.

THE OTHER DREAM JOB

As someone who relished existential conversations and had discovered the joys of self-directed growth after a dark period of my life during my teenage years, I didn't even know personal development was a thing or industry, or that working in it could be my next professional challenge. When I stumbled upon a motivational video with millions of views on Facebook, I acted on the impulse to look up the company behind it.

Much to my surprise, the company was based in my city, which is not known as a big media hub by any means. My research led me to a job postings page, where I saw no open roles that fit my wishlist. I heard a clear voice inside of me: "You're going to be the editor in chief of that publication."

Even though I've always been intuitive, (as is everyone, but social conditioning can drown out this natural tendency,) my intention to lead an authentic life got me acquainted with my intuition on a more intimate level. I now see it as a channel to infinite wisdom, a path to consciousness, an intelligence far more refined than our cognitive abilities.

For me, it shows up as an impulse so quick it's almost easy to miss, a voice that I hear clearly in my mind that stands out from my stream of consciousness, or a knowing so strong I just can't explain it. On the other hand, it never comes through as a list of pros and cons or a case of analysis paralysis.

It also lets me know when it's not time to act yet, but to hold on to an insight until inspired action shows up again, which was the case when I looked up that promising potential employer.

Inspired action did strike, prompting me to message the CEO of the company and invite him for lunch. When I met him and his cofounder, I heard the voice again: "You're going to work with them."

While we promised to keep in touch, nothing immediate came from the meeting. Notice how the unfolding of authentic living begins internally, is fueled by awareness and intuition, and takes place step by step? How it doesn't stem from forcefully trying to figure out next steps or map out an entire life revamp? Yet, through one authentic choice at a time, big magic is created.

Like the magic of sending a text message with my heart pounding, asking the cofounders whether they were open to creating a senior role for me. "Let's talk," they said. A few weeks later, I was sitting at my new desk at a job that matched all my seemingly impossible criteria, kicking off what would be two of the most transformative years of my life. And guess what? I joined as the editor-in-chief. Six months later, I became the director of operations.

THE MODELS OF THE WORLD TO UNLEARN

When you tell people you love your job so much you'd do it for free, they look at you with a mix of skepticism and awe. Or they say, "You're so lucky." Part of me understood I was lucky compared to the majority of the population, and part of me also knew there was something conscious and intentional about the process of getting the job.

And I had negotiated a better salary, more senior job title and additional time off and flexibility by being honest about my true desires and keeping my standards high even when it was scary. In a way, because I was leaving a great situation on paper, I was extra picky, which gave me the courage to truly go for what I wanted instead of making unsatisfying compromises.

All this made me wonder about the models of the world we internalize: job satisfaction vs. money, freedom vs. office job, or authenticity vs. security.

I studied journalism, not business. I was an intern for only four years before having a seat at the executive table and contributing to company-wide decisions. I had unknowingly started the process of challenging several assumptions about career, success and life, and it had a direct, unquestionable impact on my reality.

Working with like-minded people broadened my horizons even further, like when my coworker Kevin asked me: "Why not now?" when I told him I'd have my own business one day. "Because I love working here!" I answered. I was raised by entrepreneurial parents and always knew I'd become one too. But participating in established organizations was so valuable in terms of learning, teamwork and resources. Plus, I still didn't know what kind of business I wanted.

I thrived in a startup environment, which allowed me to move fast and solve problems without a lot of red tape, and wear multiple hats, which fulfilled my craving for action and variety. Our culture encouraged authenticity and vulnerability through activities such as gratitude meetings where tears were not uncommon. It helped me be more myself than ever at work and allowed for meaningful connection with my teammates.

THE PRINCIPLES THAT FOSTER AUTHENTIC SUCCESS

It's easy to throw authenticity around like a buzzword without understanding what it implies and how it's put into practice. We can add dimension to it with four concepts: awareness, intuition, vulnerability, and connection. While there is no blueprint for living on your own terms, these are guiding principles that can help you discover what that looks like for you.

Awareness

Authenticity is an inside job that begins with awareness—the state of being aware, of knowing and understanding that something is happening or exists[1]. Without first acknowledging what you want or perhaps even your confusion around what you want, how could you possibly determine what is authentic for you? The first steps are your 'bathtub moment': tuning into your feelings, observing your thoughts, noticing your actions, and paying attention to any disconnects or moments of pure flow.

Practice awareness with curiosity and compassion. It's possible that you'll notice resistance, guilt, or fear around what you uncover. A coach, therapist, or mentor can support you in this process. We don't know what we don't know, and we sometimes need tools to develop deeper self-knowledge in a constructive way. Living authentically in a society like ours is an act of radical self-love that requires courage and self-acceptance.

Intuition

Intuition is the mechanism that allows awareness to turn into authentic action. Because we are living, breathing organisms in an interconnected, ever-changing world, it's challenging to seek out rigid plans when aiming to live authentically. Externally imposed action is the antithesis to action driven from your inner guidance.

Learn what your intuition looks like and feels like. If you've been conditioned to ignore it or not to trust it, start to practice listening to it and acting on it in lower-stake settings where you feel less pressure about making a decision.

It's also eye-opening to reflect on times in your life when you followed your intuition and it paid off, what that looked like and led to, and contrast that to moments when you didn't follow your intuition.

Vulnerability

What does vulnerability have to do with authenticity? Everything. Authenticity is not always comfortable. Truths like needing to end a long-term relationship are gut-wrenching to face. When you put yourself out there in the pursuit of a desire that feels close to your heart, the fear of potential rejection or failure is amplified. Or think about how scary the idea of expressing how you truly feel or doing what you truly want can be in the face of disapproval.

Plus, authenticity will require you to trade perfection and perception-management for, at times, a messy experience in embracing your humanity.

Connection

It's brave to look at everything that makes you you, and to challenge some of it. It's even braver to share yourself. For example, when I realized I had replaced risky behavior like substance abuse with high-achievement, it poked holes in my identity. When I opened up about traumatic memories, I could barely make eye contact. But the more I did it, the more profound my connection to myself and others became.

On your own authenticity journey, you might discover things that you perceive to be less desirable about yourself and feel shame. Being willing to go there can bring discomfort, but, with self-compassion, it can make you fall in love with yourself.

When interacting with others from an authentic space, you'll notice relationship dynamics change. People tend to receive authenticity with relief, as it's a cue that they're in a safe space where they too can drop facades. But others might be dealing with too much shame to do so, and protect themselves by rejecting vulnerability when triggered by your authenticity. Know that this has nothing to do with you.

Expression

These four guiding principles culminate in the beautiful, glorious expression of your unique nature. From speaking your truth to allowing your career to become a shape-shifting container for your multiple facets and strengths, authentic expression is the outwards projection of your inner world.

When your thoughts, feelings, and actions are congruent, and when your choices are in line with your values, you are on the path of living a truly authentic life and reaping its rewards. And it's supposed to be continuously evolving, as you are not static and neither is the world you're a part of.

THE LIFELONG JOURNEY AND DAILY PRACTICES

This evolution can become completely disruptive to life as you know it. I discovered that a lot of my old wants were driven by trauma and maladaptive coping strategies as I sought to fill a void or craved safety and control. There were layers to it.

As I expanded my consciousness, my inner guidance allowed more unfolding to take place. I quit my full-time job to start my own business (without a blueprint, of course!).

I am now a multi-passionate entrepreneur, writer, and career mentor who stopped thinking herself wrong for having multiple interests and skills. The best part? My projects, which include being the founder of a content marketing agency, mentoring others so they can tap into their authentic power, and advising business leaders, are an amalgamation of my values and a playground to explore my gifts and purpose. It's no coincidence. I did, after all, muster the courage to ask myself important questions, and allowed some answers to drive my decisions without letting a lack of answers keep me stuck.

ABOUT THE AUTHOR

ANOUARE ABDOU

Anouare Abdou is a writer, entrepreneur and career mentor who believes that successful careers can be vehicles for authentic self-expression and that it's time for a major paradigm shift in the way we create, change and uphold systems.

Whether she's advising executives as a management consultant, leading her team as a content marketing agency founder, writing about personal development or guiding 1-on-1 clients, she is obsessed with helping people and organizations thrive.

Instagram: https://www.instagram.com/anouare_a/
Email: anouare@seeksolveconsulting.com

2

ASHLEY GENE PINKERTON

WITH THE SPARK OF ONE, THE FLAME IS LIT

"Success" was written as a note on my wall, a bookmark, holding the place of where to begin again. As I pondered what I would write here, in this chapter, in this sharing of my story— my Success Code—I remembered with a burst of insight just how much this word "success" has influenced and impacted my life, aligning me as the woman I am today.

It was the first months of my awakening, of my sobriety, and the taking back of my power. I'll tell you, in those early days, I needed those subtle reminders; the signs and signals that showed me the way, that supported my path to self-empowerment, discovery and soulful embodiment. These little notes became the sparks that lit the flames of my heart, affirming that my success was imminent.

This word, written simply in the script of my sister, Mackenzie—my fiercest ally, my best friend who stood by me through the tests and trials of life—invoked something within me, commanding from me a determination that carried me through those very raw moments, as I peeled back the layers of my programing in search of who I was meant to be. Each time I saw it, each time I walked past it hanging on my wall or opened the book where it sat as a place marker, it reminded me that *this was the outcome;* that I would succeed beyond a shadow of a doubt. Still to this day, I keep this note inside my wallet, shining back at me, it reminds me of where I came from and where I am headed.

What does it even mean to be successful? The answer has shifted for me so many times throughout the years. As a little girl, playing in the forest, dreaming up entire worlds and realities with my best friend, Missy, my measure of success was directly proportional to how many hours a day were spent playing. Growing up aligned with such imagination, we were able to create and make believe for hours and even days on end. As we got older, we were told we were too old to play; and the worst part was we believed them. What once was held as a measure of success began to fade away; the definition shifted into something external, something that was more about physical things than emotional feelings of joyful expression and wellbeing. As the years went on and I stepped into adulthood, this new definition shaped my reality, and in the midst of it, I lost myself.

How had it gotten to this point? I had done everything society had told me to do. I had done my best to be "a good girl". I graduated high school with decent grades, I had a job, I went to college. Shit, I was even dating one of the popular guys from high school *(jackpot, right?!)* and yet, I was totally miserable. Are you telling me that I got the recipe for success wrong? Which ingredient did I miss? I felt like the walking dead, my passion squashed and my soul silenced by the mind numbing choices I picked day after day. I was continuously looking outside of myself for the next fix, the next thing that might bring me some sort of happiness, and so many nights were spent looking for relief at the bottom of a bottle. But that's what people did, right? After all, I was surrounded by them: the same regulars at the bar night after night.

How many of us are sleeping away our lives, living a nightmare, never recognizing the fullest potential that exists within us? This was me, consumed by my external search for alignment, that in a sea of people, I was a bit of everyone and I was nowhere to be found. For so long, I had felt alone, like a stranger living in my own life. The people around me looked familiar, though the woman in the mirror looking back at me I no longer recognized, and the little girl who once imagined, believed, and dreamed her world into being was a ghost of my forgotten past.

I knew I had come to this Earth for something special, *for so much more than what I was limiting myself to.* And although I was doing everything I was told to do, I was sick and locked in the depths of depression and suffering of which I wouldn't wish upon anyone. I remember looking at myself in the mirror at what I had become and thinking, "This is not what I came here to do! I am meant for so much more!" It seems like after that declaration, after that realization of something more that was calling me forward, my awakening began. My power of will was restored and my willingness to let go of what had once defined me became the catalyst for my transformation. It was the end of 2012, and it was as if a switch flipped. I knew there was no turning back, and there was only forward motion into alignment with my soul and the reasons I had chosen to be here. At that moment, *I chose to live.*

After so many years of misaligned action and external focus, the journey to look within was absolutely terrifying. Having to face down all your demons, all the lies, the deceit—the choices I had made—it took every ounce of my courage. When I first went within and dropped into my heart, all I saw was darkness; my light was buried in the rubble of my past choices. I immersed myself in books, reading everything I could that would help me to know what to do, where to look, who I could rely on, and how to break through to the other side of me. In those first two years, I read at least fifty books, and knowledge became my guiding light. One of my most pivotal influences, a self-help book called *Spiritual Growth: Being Your Higher Self* changed my life forever and gave me the tools I needed to connect with the truths of my soul, the divine counterpart within me, and my Higher Self that had all the answers and walked the path before me. I learned how to draw down this energy, to summon forth the endless support of love and light, of our higher-level guides, and I began to call this into my life day in and day out.

The more I connected with Mother Earth, with my light and with love, the more my gifts awakened, and I began to find my way into alignment with my destiny. The realization of my healing gifts, my connection to my Higher Power, to the sacred Mother Earth, and all my allies, (the plants, animals, and crystals) began to solidify my knowing and understanding that healing came from within. It arose from my alignment with myself, not from a pill or substance or person or program. It is a way of being, a decision to live and to no longer wither way.

As I prayed for a solution, Energy Medicine came as an answer. It began with me finding Reiki, a healing technique of the laying on of hands that originated in Japan. Through the activation of this energy within me, I was able to call forth the infinite flow of light and life force that surrounds us in each moment, and I began to channel it for healing: both my own healing as well as my family, friends and clients. Reiki opened the door to my calling, and it was through countless synchronicities that I came to find my soul's truest call as a Medicine Woman. In fact, from that moment on, all of the most magical alignments on my path can be tracked back to that original Google search for "Reiki Masters near me" and from there, synchronicity paved the path to my Highest Self.

My insatiable search for more guided me to *The Four Winds Society*, an institute of Shamanic Energy Medicine. This opened me to a whole new reality and provided solutions to free myself and those I knew I was here to serve. Considered a modern-day mystery school and anchored in the indigenous wisdom teachings of lineages from South America, The Four Winds helped me to reclaim my power and wholeness in a way that transformed my life forever. Up until this point, I had been guiding myself through my spiritual awakening; but here in the company of my fellow students, guided by our mentors and teachers, I came home to myself once and for all. Though the initiation ushered forth in those many months together, I learned how to transform my suffering and the triggers of my past traumas into the very medicine that would propel me forward. What had once been my greatest challenges became my most potent strengths, and the qualifications that would assist me in walking others home to themselves, just as I had done.

On the Shamanic path, one learns to transcend limitations; one learns to face the deepest darkness with courage and integrity. It is a scary thing to go within that sorrow, to see oneself in the shadow, and take inventory of all we have become. It is so essential, so necessary, for if one doesn't see and know them, these hidden aspects will once again consume us. There is often a common misconception, that assumes all that is found in the shadow is of darkness, but what I have found is that some of the most radiant aspects of Soul, of my light, were once hidden in my shadow.

By burning down and releasing the roles that kept me bound to what society said I needed to be, I became available to this moment, able to answer the Call of Spirit that allowed me to accept my seat in the lineage of creation, remembering my potential as a creator of my reality and as a catalyst of change as a leader and in my service to humanity. With the past no longer dictating my presence in the now, I was able to bring liberation to myself, to my family, to my bloodline and to the heart and soul of the collective. It was in these defining moments that I came to realize what a profound impact my own personal healing would have on those around me; that by remembering myself, I helped others to remember as well.

After my training, I came to understand just how much my early years, the way I felt, and the depression and the addiction I had recovered from had been governed by my empathic sensitivity and misalignment with myself. I had never been taught about empathy before my awakening. I hadn't been taught about the fundamentals of energetics and how deeply connected we all are to each other. Because of this and taking on the energy of others through my feeling of the collective, I was not able to find myself or able to discern what was mine and what wasn't mine. Through the tools cultivated in my experiences of going within myself, aligning with my Higher Self, working with energy and being able to discern what was mine and what wasn't, I began to walk my Soul Aligned Path and to guide my clients through similar transformations.

Through the guidance of Master Teachers such as Abraham-Hicks, I began to understand the true meaning of our emotions and began to see them as a "Guidance System", our internal GPS helping us to navigate our alignment. I became aware of the power of my focus and that I could choose the thoughts I was thinking. I learned that my ability to shift my focus and thought pattern to one that brought relief and empowerment allowed me to maintain my alignment and brought me freedom from the heavy emotions I had once been plagued by. I began to realize, at an even deeper level, that the addiction that once ran rampant in my life had been a symptom of my misalignment and disconnection from my Higher Self. Instead of looking outside of myself, as I once had, I now looked within—and in doing so, I found the true freedom and ecstasy of connection.

In working at the energetic level, at the level of the soul and the emotions, we are able to create change at a quantum level, shifting our perspective and moving energy at the speed of light. As a client once told me, "I have received more out of this two hour session with you than I have from thirty years of therapy." Think of the implications of this: *two hours of focus and intention vs thirty years of weekly sessions!!* I don't say this to discount the power of therapy as I, too, have received much value from therapy at points in my life. I share this only to bring forth a different perspective: that as we work in the energy, engaged with the soul to transcend how something lives within us now, we rewrite the story of our past and shift the trajectory of our future, inviting ourselves to be embodied as the true gift in the present breath of now. As we transcend the limitations which once bound us to the past and to the emotions connected to it, we bring true liberation to our soul.

The solution is simple, so simple that most will overlook it, just as I once did. It starts with a desire, a decision; a willingness to close our eyes, to take some breaths, to drop into the heart and to go within. The key components to our liberation are simpler than one might realize: a favorite place in nature, bare feet on the ground, a few deep breaths into the body, and the courage to discover what is tucked inside. In getting to know ourselves and establishing a strong connection to our Higher Self, our body and our guides, we can then more easily distinguish between what is ours and what isn't ours. Through these tools of discernment, we can release what doesn't belong to us and get to know who we are in our essence.

Through the path of my spiritual initiation, what I found of success circled me back to the perspective I held as a young girl. Success is connection; it is playful; it is light. It is alignment with our soul, with our passion, with what we came here to do and be, and the impact we came to make. It is an embodiment of our gifts, of our wisdom and of the mastery that our soul carries. This is why, even though some have achieved great success in their career, work, and so on, they may still feel unfulfilled. Success is not tied to things and statuses. It is deeply rooted and connected to our alignment with who we really are at a Higher Self/Soul level. Success is our ability to experience joy, to use our imagination and to see through the eyes of childlike wonder; to believe in the possibility hidden within the Great Mystery and to dance with it. Success is being in the flow state, where synchronicity after synchronicity leads us forward; "the bread crumbs" from the Higher Self, as I like to call them, are the signs letting us know we are hot on the trail of our truth.

When we stop for a moment and recognize how powerful that is, *how powerful we are* when we align ourselves with the passion that exists within our hearts; when we allow ourselves to be carried forward by this momentum; this call to show up, to fully express ourselves as the best version of who we are meant to be; we align ourselves with success. It is asking each of us to remember who we are. It is asking for our collaboration and co-creation together, to not only empower one but *to empower all* and reach beyond the veil of limitations and into the light of infinite potential.

The question then is what are we waiting for? Who are we waiting for? *Because we are the only ones with the power to change our lives individually and collectively.*

It is our own light that ignites the hearts of the world, that ripples out to touch all of those who are open to receive and ready to live. There is no limit to what we are capable of when we align and allow the wisdom of the heart to guide us.

In our modern way of doing things, we have lost sight of our interconnectedness to every aspect of existence. We have forgotten how integral our presence is in guiding forward a more aligned way of being, one which allows us to walk in *ayni*, in right relationship with all of life, uniquely expressing our individuality, while honoring our unity and connection to each other. When we recognize that we are each unique musical notes, and that as we come together in harmony, we create a masterpiece in the greatest symphony ever written, with each of us having a significant place in this orchestra we call life. If just one of us is missing, then the rest of this creation cannot reach its full potential.

It is our life experience that initiates us, that brings forth our qualifications in our service to others and to the highest good. As we carry forward these gifts, we give birth to a New Way, to the New Earth where all of life is honored and seen as sacred. From this higher perspective, from this alignment with our Soul we see that life is a ceremony and our presence is offering.

It is my prayer that from this you carry forth the codes to activate your success and the soulful embodiment that sets your heart on fire. I hold the door open for each of us to step through. Won't you come with me?

ABOUT THE AUTHOR

ASHLEY GENE PINKERTON

Ashley Gene Pinkerton is a New Earth Medicine Woman, Intuitive Sound Healer, and Soul Alignment Coach. Her driving force is to be a teacher and guide of a more heart centered, Soul embodied way of being that allows us to live in harmony in all areas of our life.

Weaving together techniques of shamanism, sound healing, energy medicine and laser coaching, she assists her clients in rewriting the map of their lives, allowing them to reclaim their power, wholeness, and aligning them with their Soul's highest calling.

She offers customized 1:1 coaching and healing sessions, online programs and global ceremonial retreats.

Ashley's spiritual awakening in 2012 was the catalyst to her transformation, aligning her with the trajectory of her Soul's mission and all she shares today.

In 2017 Ashley published her first book, *Spiraling Forward*, a collection of her personal poetry and musings on love, light and life.

Link Tree: https://linktr.ee/ashleygene
Website: www.ashleygeneofficial.com
Instagram: https://www.instagram.com/ashley_gene_official/
Facebook: https://www.facebook.com/ashley.gene.pinkerton/

3

CARLY FERGUSON

LET YOUR TRUTH BE YOUR IDENTITY

*S*uccess can be found in every truthful moment that you live. You can be successful right now if you choose to be —right now!

I've only just come to learn after my forty years in this body, that being successful is really a spiritual and mental state. It has absolutely nothing to do with status or wealth or achievements. If you're living your truth, then you can't help but be successful, even if it looks different to what everyone else is doing. But the problem is that the majority of us have been trained to be the opposite of who we are in order to fit in.

Slowly, over so many years that we hardly notice it happening, we abandon the precious parts of us that make up exactly who we came here to be.

This is exactly why I've made it my life's mission to support and facilitate the awakening of individuals to their own truth. To help strip away the professional identities and masks that we wear in an attempt to fit in.

It's my wish for everyone to surrender to their own uniqueness and understand that their human design is the perfect design for them. Living in alignment with that will bring more joy, peace and abundance than you could ever imagine—just by living your truth. Sounds easy, right? Too easy? Easy is right. Start believing in it.

Enough is enough. Are you f*cking ready to get truthful with yourself? Are you ready to throw everything you thought you had to be out of the window, and get back to you—the real you? I mean the 'you' before all of that conditioning you received in childhood and throughout your education, those expectations put on you, and the expectations that you consciously or unconsciously put on yourself. The real damn you.

See, the systems we live and work in don't want us to be ourselves; they don't want us to challenge the norm, to question the way things are done. Individuality doesn't benefit them. The command and control approach, the hierarchical structures, the processes and methodologies, these organizations run like machines. They need us to simply be cogs that run smoothly. Expressing individuality has been frowned upon because it's seen as disruptive. Truthfulness is seen as a rebellious act in the workplace. This is where a lot of the suppression of *my* truth came from as I worked in the corporate world. I was afraid to express my individuality, I was being trained to be the opposite of who I was, and it didn't feel good.

My career spans twenty years, and in that time I've been a TV researcher, a TV runner and assistant director, a talent agent, an admin assistant, marketing manager and director, a consultant, and now an executive coach and human design expert. I also have many other unrelated projects that I'm working on. This might seem chaotic to some. I once would have agreed with you, but I know now that I'm simply a renaissance woman, a polymath, a manifesting generator, a gemini; I'm a multi-passionate person who is here to do and achieve many diverse things and I do so in my own messy way. I'm emotional, I speak my truth as I think it, I change my mind a lot, I hardly ever finish a book, and I prefer to be in a supporting role rather than in the limelight. I try to embrace all of these parts of me every day and work them into my business strategy. The more I embrace my truth and allow this to be my identity as opposed to fighting it or projecting a fake one, the more successful I feel.

I was thirty-five when the realization hit that I'd been going about success all wrong. After a series of work incidents where I was told to be more of this or less of that, I found myself trying so hard to 'get it right' and attempt to fit into others' expectations of me that I stopped trusting myself. When we stop trusting our inner authority and instead start listening more to others, we disconnect from our truth.

In September of 2016, while working for an American software start-up in London, I suffered burnout. I spent much of my personal time crying, drinking wine, eating pastries, and drinking full fat lattes on my lunch break. My acne was on overdrive, I'd gained some weight, my social life was surface level, and my love life a disaster. As I crossed the road in busy London on my 20 minute lunch break, I had a near miss with a motorcycle and found myself daydreaming about it wiping me out so I could enjoy a short hospital stay and be looked after. I didn't want to die; I just wanted a break from the fast lane. On the outside, it looked like I was thriving: achieving success in my role, buying expensive handbags with my bonus, filling up my bank account, flying to glamorous places for work, and working my way up the corporate ladder. But the professional mask I was wearing wasn't a true reflection of who I really was deep down. I didn't feel like being me was enough for anyone.

As I crept towards my breakdown, the real me started to break through, but all of that pent up frustration of trying so damn hard to hide my natural gifts and personality meant that it all came out as anger and emotional frustration. I couldn't keep up the pretense anymore. I hated my job, I hated the people I was working with, I hated the office environment, I hated the fakeness, I hated the suppression of me, I hated the direction my career was going in, I hated being told what to do, how to behave, how to dress, how to think.....I hated it all. I didn't like the me that was starting to surface, but inevitably it needed to come out in order for me to move through the emotions I was suppressing.

The truth is uncomfortable. No one wants to hear or see it. I was crying out for help, and that raw vulnerability made the people I was working with back away. They just wanted me to behave and do as I was told. When we parted, I felt relieved, ecstatic, and free...as well as ashamed, embarrassed, scared, rejected. What do I do now? My bank account said I was successful but I was unhappy and unfulfilled on the inside. I gave notice on my London flat rental and moved back in with my parents. I quickly booked a flight to Australia for six weeks and then volunteered for a charity in Borneo for three months. This wasn't yet the beginning of my recovery though. It would take time before I would learn that running away from your truth doesn't fix the problem. What came next was a long journey of reclaiming all of the parts of me I had been denying for so long. It was time to do things on my terms. To have truth be my identity, not the one imposed on me.

For most of my career, I attempted to conform. I championed everyone else's individuality but denied my own. I questioned my instincts and abandoned my natural preferences and gifts. Part of the problem was that I lacked role models who I could identify with, so I thought that to progress my career, I had to be more like the people I could see at the top: confident and thick skinned, rational, logical and good public speakers. I had to talk less, toughen up, be more professional, feel less. Dress a certain way, say this, don't say that.

I clearly remember being told by a senior leader whom I respected that I didn't display the leadership qualities necessary to be on the leadership team. When I asked what those qualities looked like, he told me to look at my male counterparts and be more like them. How on earth are we meant to trust ourselves and show up authentically when we are given advice like that by leaders we're supposed to look up to?

Is it any wonder that many of us suffer from a crisis of identity mid-career? We've been contorted and tweaked and conditioned so much that we've forgotten who we are. The mini traumas we experience in the workplace when we are just being ourselves range from being told off to ignored or rejected, and are what cause us to stop trusting ourselves. **Finding our way back to ourselves is our success code.**

The truth is, there is no one way to be successful and no one-size-fits-all approach to working and leading. Reconnecting with and reclaiming the parts of me that I'd abandoned and denied are what I've found to be my personal success codes, and they can be for you too. No mentor, role model, business program, or self-help book is going to be able to give you the exact recipe for success. Trust that your way *is* the right way.

Everything that you've been told are your flaws and weaknesses over the years are actually your greatest gifts in disguise. When you deny these, it doesn't matter how outwardly successful you become; it won't mean a thing if you're out of integrity with yourself.

So how can you begin to flip your perceived flaws into success codes?

Here's how I flipped some of mine:

'I am too emotional.'
'I care deeply about the importance of my work and impact on the world. My passion is what fuels projects and gets stuff done in a timely manner.'

'I'm too sensitive.'
'My psychic abilities mean that I sense what others need so that I can help them.'

'I'm disruptive.'

'I challenge the status quo because it's part of my purpose; to improve the way we do things for the better for the collective.'

'I move too quickly.'
'I'm here to achieve many things and I can handle the speed required for that.'

'I change my mind too much.'
'I trust my instincts and am able to pivot when required.'

'I'm too informal/unprofessional.'
'By unapologetically being myself in business, I inspire others to be their most authentic selves too.'

Exercise
Grab a pen and paper and write down a list of your perceived flaws, the things people have told you that you need to change about yourself, and flip them into your own personal success codes.

Now the key is to start believing these statements at a deep cellular level. This isn't a job interview exercise where you're trying to sell your flaws to someone else. This is about you believing that your flaws are your greatest gifts.

It can be easy to override your own instincts and ignore your gifts when you're told over and over your weaknesses are to be improved on. People managers have a huge responsibility to nurture their employees' gifts and not suffocate them, but unfortunately this is a common occurrence. I've been guilty of this myself in the past, and I would like to take this opportunity to apologize to anyone who I've managed or mentored before I woke up to my own conditioning. We have to become aware of this collectively and start allowing everyone to live their truth. Conscious leadership and coaching may be the solution while providing guidance for the more technical skills.

I truly believe in the intuitive power of my clients. I *could* teach them what worked for me, but I know that each client ultimately knows deep down what they need to do. What I do is help clear away any blocks to clarity and cultivate the energy needed to act and move forward. This is what the best managers do too. In fact, we should abolish the title of 'manager' and just replace it with 'coach'. We could all benefit from learning how to ask each other really good questions, and stop telling each other what to do from your own perspective. Your way is not necessarily their way.

One of my most important discoveries in my role as a coach and teacher has been human design. Human design is the study of our energetic auras, a guide for how we're meant to most powerfully utilize our energy in the world and how we're wired to make decisions, as well as a blueprint highlighting our inherent gifts. It combines wisdom from astrology, Kabbalah, the Hindu-Brahmin chakra system, the I Ching, and quantum physics. It's also known as the Science of Differentiation which highlights the uniqueness and individuality of each person while also stressing the importance that when we live our unique designs, we thrive together collectively.

The evolution of organizations is going in the right direction, one where the importance of creating and cultivating an environment that feels safe to bring your whole self to work is being seen as an important part of business strategy. There are many leaders consciously creating businesses just like this that allow each individual to focus on their gifts and work in a way that aligns with their own unique way of working. This makes my heart sing.

I am so glad for younger people entering the workforce in this era who are having their first work experience in a place that allows them to be themselves. But for those who have been stung like me by the curse of the machine, and have lost touch with their true self, human design is a perfect way to start to uncover the forgotten parts of yourself.

The first time I saw my human design BodyGraph I was confused. It looked like a complicated map that I could never navigate. But once I started to study mine, it felt like coming home. Essentially what I was seeing was a manual for me. I quickly started to experiment with two specific things in my blueprint. The first thing I learned was that my strategy as a Manifesting Generator is 'waiting to respond'. I looked back at all of the times I had tried to make something happen, and the times I had been in the hustle versus the times I'd let opportunities flow to me naturally. When I really thought about it, all of my best opportunities had come from nowhere. I gave myself permission to stop the hustle, and the results were instant.

The second thing I experimented with was my decision making authority which is 'emotional'. Because I make decisions based on how things make me feel, and because I create my own emotional wave, I need to give myself more time before making a decision. New sentences I started to use were: 'Let me come back to you on that,' or, 'I'll sleep on it'. The *manifestor* part of me wants to say yes to everything, but I now know that this is what causes an overcommitment of energy to the wrong things and regrets later on.

I started to practice reading Human Design BodyGraphs with my friends and family and then with my clients. The results were undeniable. There were tears of relief from some, in recognition of what they'd known all along but resisted because they felt there was something wrong with them. It's an honour to do.

Once you embrace all of the parts of you that you thought were flaws, you can start to build them into a strategy for your career or business. Your human design blueprint essentially offers you a manual for yourself and how you best work. It's full of treasure and information that you can use to your advantage. Connect the dots, and you will have your own personal success strategy.

Please know this: there is nothing wrong with you and you don't need to be anything but yourself in order to be successful. Release the pressure to change or be something you're not. Simply be you as your perfect true self.

Your creative process, your strategy, your daily routine, your decision-making, your ideas, and your unique way of expressing and sharing your gifts are all right.

This should be part of every new starter induction in the workplace, as should human design. Every leader should make it part of their responsibility to not only lead from a place of true identity themselves, but also encourage their team to do the same every day.

Celebrate the unique brilliance of you and everyone you ever work with. **Let truth be your identity. That is your success code.**

Exercise
I'll leave you with some final questions and prompts to ponder on.

- Remember a time when you could really be yourself at work and didn't need to act or look the part in any way
- Did being fully yourself change anything about your work?
- What conditions were in place that helped you to be fully yourself at work?
- What sides of you that you LOVE come out when you feel safe and at ease?
- What are you not being honest with yourself/others about?
- Describe your perfect work week if no one was watching?
- What expectations are you ready to let go of?

'Sat Nam'

(*Translation* - 'Truth is my essence' or 'I am truth')

Carly x

ABOUT THE AUTHOR

CARLY FERGUSON

Carly Ferguson is an Executive Coach and Human Design Specialist who helps leaders, solopreneurs, founders and their teams identify their innate strengths and bring their ambitious business and career visions into 3D.

Carly began her career in the TV industry and has spent over ten years in the corporate world, leading marketing teams and transformation programs for FTSE 250 companies. In this time, Carly realized she has a gift for seeing beyond individuals' perceived limitations and helping them to see their flaws as their greatest gifts, so that they could step into their full potential and personal power.

Through coaching and human design, Carly helps her clients to find the peace, satisfaction and abundance that comes when you work and lead in line with your true nature.

Carly is based in the UK and works remotely with clients all over the world.

Website: https://www.carly-ferguson.com
Instagram: https://www.instagram.com/carlyfergusoncoaching/
Email: carly@carly-ferguson.com

4

CHANTEL PORTER

SUCCESS IS FOUND IN THE WILD

I am a woman,
Woman of the wild.
Free unto herself.
Daughter of the moon,
Keeper of the Womb.
The Wild calls to me,
In the darkness of the night.
It is my initiation,
My freedom from conditioning.
Releasing me from the cage.
Anchored into my womb,
I become one with every womb,
With Earth's Wild Womb.
I am a Woman of the Wild,
Woman of the Womb
-Chantel Porter

S uccess to me is found in the wild, in connecting to the wild nature that society has forbidden, shamed, and locked away. This kind of Wild will radically transform you, push you through all your fears and will set your life on fire, putting you into flow with your own soul's purpose. As I have come to know it now, success is living life in a way that fills your own soul, putting down what we've been told has to be and picking up what is true and right for your unique soul. That kind of success brings joy, fulfillment, connection and passion into your every waking moment.

Success is not at all what we have been told it is; in fact, it's everything we have been told it is *not*! Because of what we have been taught, we have forgotten to honor our wild nature that directly leads to human souls who are thriving and full of purpose and light. To be wild means no longer living caged and in captivity, allowing your whole self to be free, to be seen, untamed and undomesticated. Free of restraints and societal expectations, wild and free the way we were meant to be. So caught up in climbing the ladder upwards, we have lost our way to our own personal wilderness; but that *is* where our unique success codes can be found. We've lost our ability to anchor downwards into our womb, into the earth, and into our feminine crown; this is our Solar Plexus, Sacral and Root chakras because we have been taught to be in our heads, being in ego, it's celebrated. But within our feminine nature, we can find we were never meant to be the egoic robots that society has conditioned us to be, or to fit into the box that was set in front of us. Instead of up and out, we need to go down and in. This is where the wild is found.

Thinking back on the things I was told that my life could or couldn't be is overwhelming at times, especially when I look at my daughter and I cannot imagine ever telling her the things I was told. If you came from a low-income family or from the foster care system, maybe the same is true for you. Maybe you were told similar limiting beliefs that programmed what you thought you could achieve or were worthy of having. I can still hear their voices, telling me I would never amount to anything. Don't dream too high because you'll never get there; you're the daughter of a single teen mom from a broken home; the daughter of a drug dealer; on and on and on I heard their voices, "Beggars can't be choosers." I heard people tell me all the time that kids who come from where I did don't get out. They don't usually amount to anything so don't try and that my life would always be a struggle.

I was born to a teen mom who had herself been raised in a very damaging environment. She suffered an extent of physical and mental abuse that no person ever should. There was also poverty, alcohol and substance abuse resulting in severe trauma that I will probably never know of the full breadth. She was just sixteen when I was born, and I was her second child. My brother was almost one when I was born, and I can only imagine how greatly this impacted her life, and mine. There is a stigma that is set upon you when you become a single mom at any age, not to mention being a teenager from a low-income family that already has abuse and addiction running through it. When my mother was younger, I'm not sure anyone around her understood what generational trauma was or how to help her. She had, and I am sure still does, a fire in her that cannot be tamed—as do I. Many people throughout my life have tried to put that fire out, telling me that it and I weren't acceptable. My place was to be quiet, soft, submissive, pretty, bear children, and accept my place in this world. That is the kind of "successful life" I was entitled to, and in a way my life was already written for me. I saw all the sad faces staring at me like I was a wounded animal that was not worth saving; everywhere I went there were always these pitiful or disgusted faces. People waited for my mistakes, they expected all the failures, and waited around just to remind me that I would never be anything more and that I could never have what others have. I needed to find a man to take care of me, even if I wasn't happy with him. To fulfill my duty as a woman, to have children and do what I was made for.

These voices and programming swirled around inside me like tidal waves trying to put out my fire, to drown out my soul. This point was driven home by an aunt's husband at the time, when I was sixteen and at a family gathering, he said to me: "So, when are you going to start popping out babies, cause you've got those baby makin' hips!" I can still remember where I was, how uncomfortable I felt, and how I wanted to crawl out of my skin and run away. That was my lot in life; that was the "success" I was allowed to strive for; that was my place in this world, and so I better just accept it. I began to believe my place in this world was to struggle. That I couldn't have what others did, and my actions and choices became a self-fulfilling prophecy of these beliefs. Hello generational trauma and limiting beliefs!

I've always struggled *hard* to conform, to follow the plan that I was given. We aren't "supposed" to find this out, but something within me knew we were *never* meant to conform, because we were always meant to run wild. A fire was raging inside of me that I had no idea how to control or what to do with, yet. I continued to make people uncomfortable and push the boundaries. I refused to force myself into the box or labels that were placed on me. I was too "big" to fit inside society's ideal of a woman. For so long I had no idea how to use this fire the way my soul was meant to. I operated as my shadow/false self, like a volcano erupting and destroying everything in my path. I decided very early on in my life that I would prove everyone wrong and become everything they said that I couldn't and wouldn't. Even if it meant killing myself on the inside, even if it meant sacrificing my mental health, my energy and my time with my daughter.

I defied all the odds and went to college, obtaining three separate diplomas, one of which I began when my daughter was five months old. I remember I was still breastfeeding while going to school, and during the day the milk would build up and leak out without my control. I would have to take breaks to go to the washroom so I could express some of it in order to relieve the pressure and pain. I hated it! I hated being away from my daughter all day when she was so young, and when I would pick her up she would all but attack my breasts in order to nurse. She hated bottles; nursing had always worked for her and I. It was a beautiful time that I cherished, but I eventually had to stop because it became too uncomfortable to continue while being in college.

These kinds of "sacrifices" would continue for her and I because I fell into the trap of working harder and harder to prove myself at my job, to my clients, to myself and to my boss, only to have very little left for her at the end of the day. I was battling my trauma pretty hard during the first few years of her life and that didn't help. I was always trying to go higher and be more, so much so that I ended up working for myself and taking on business seven days a week. I was so desperate to reach what I was told I couldn't have, disguising it as "hustling" or "working hard" to get to something better, that I didn't realize how much this was killing us both. When I look back on that woman now, I don't even recognize her. She was barely surviving; she was the walking dead, but to look at her you would never guess. She was well put together, make-up always done, hair always done, nails, nice clothes. Looking back now, I can see how much I was trying to prove something I was never meant to prove. I was carrying pain, beliefs and programming that weren't mine to carry; they weren't mine to believe.

One day though, something changed. Through doing work as an esthetician, I was fortunate enough to meet some of the most amazing women on this earthly planet that still to this day support me and cheer me on. One of them introduced me to a book called *The Miracle Morning* by Hal Elrod. This book started a cascade of changes that nobody ever could have predicted or would have expected. It flipped me upside down and shook me out. It was the catalyst to the work that I do now. I will forever be grateful to this woman and this book. I have read hundreds of books since then, but that one will always be *the* book I'll always remember.

Since then, my life has unfurled in the most beautiful ways. After reading Hal's book, I changed everything I was doing. I changed how I was thinking, how I was speaking and acting. How I interacted with my daughter began to morph and we began to flourish together. I started setting boundaries with my work and my time. I read as many books as I would get my hands on and I took programs to learn how to get more of what I was feeling, to heal more of what needed healing, and as I sat one morning in my morning practice that literally saved *and* changed my life, the tears came flowing down my face because I didn't know that I could feel that good. I didn't know I could feel the peace I was feeling, or the gratitude for my life. That last one was a *biggie* for me, It was something I don't think I had truly ever felt before then. I knew very quickly that I wanted *every* woman possible to feel what I was feeling, to show her that what she needed was inside of her. That is where my work began, guiding women home to themselves and their bodies, showing them how to feel safe and trust in themselves and their bodies, to find their inner Wild Woman so they can be free of the programming, trauma, and conditioning they've endured.

We all have a special Wild woman inside of us that we are meant to embody only in the way *we* can. There is only one you in this entire world and that means that what will make your unique life a success is just meant for you. It most certainly isn't found in the "hustle"; your success is found in the Wild, in your Wild. To be Wild is to live in a state of nature, where you are untamed and undomesticated. Truly as you were meant to be, free of the restraints of society's expectations of success and being, free of others' beliefs, and free of conditioning. Just wild and free, that is where your magick and your own unique success codes are to be found. I don't want another woman of this world to think she cannot have everything she deserves and desires. I want you to know that success should be defined on *your* terms. What you achieve in your life should be based on what calls to you and lights you the F up inside! I've come to know success as living my life as my authentic self. Listening to the calls of the wild within that guide me to living my life with passion, joy, and love. Being of service in the world for the greater good and making an impact with my work "for the good of all or not at all".

We have been so caught up in climbing "the ladder" upwards that we have forgotten to honor our feminine energy, we have lost our ability to anchor downwards into the earth, into our feminine crown and our magick. We must go from up and out to down and in, and this is where we can find our success codes. The Wild earth can heal us if we allow her to, if we spend time with her, dig our feet in, and receive all she has to offer. She is the medicine that will cleanse your soul and bring you back home.

Below I have included an earthing ritual to help guide you home to Mother Earth and to your soul. This ritual can be used daily to center yourself, connect with the earth, release stress, worry or anxiety, or to simply quiet your monkey mind and find your intuition and inner voice. The more we connect with her, the more grounded into ourselves we become.

With Wild Love,
Chantel

Earthing Ritual

Earthing is the process of connecting to the Earth's energy by standing or sitting on the earth and putting your barefoot on the earth in the grass or sand. You can also do this standing or sitting against a tree while putting your feet to the earth. After a few minutes of connection, the healing and loving effects of the earth's balanced energy are undeniable. When we feel lost, afraid and unsafe in the world, connecting and communing with her can bring you home.

Begin by finding a quiet place in nature where you will not be disturbed. Spend 2-3 minutes breathing deeply, focusing on the inhale and exhale, or do 4 cycle breaths. This is breathing for 4 seconds in, holding for 4 seconds, and releasing for 4 seconds., Do this for a total of 4 times. Make sure that on the exhale, you let it all out.

Bring your attention to your feet, and visualize roots growing down into the ground from the bottoms of your feet. Feel and visualize in your mind's eye the roots growing deeper, past all the layers of the earth, the layers of rock, until it reaches the core of Mother Earth.

Stop here and feel your connection to the energy of the Earth. Release anything you wish to be free of into the core of the earth. Imagine it all pouring into her through the roots. Begin drawing the Earth's healing, positive and loving energy back up into you with each breath. Imagine the loving energy flowing up through you and back down into the earth, filling you up until you're filled up with loving, healing energy in every cell of your body; imagine this as white light energy vibrating through you. Then push that energy out to encompass your body and aura.

Bask in this energy here and breathe deeply for a few moments or minutes. When you are ready, wiggle your fingers and toes, open your eyes, and come back to the present. Finish by thanking Mother Earth for this time and exchange.

ABOUT THE AUTHOR

CHANTEL PORTER

Chantel Porter is known as a Keeper of the Womb. She started Wild Woman Magick to guide women who struggled with cultural conditioning and generational and sexual trauma as she once had. Through Shamanic medicine and energy healing, she guides women back home to their bodies, cycles, and wild nature. Chantel began this work after finding, in her own

healing journey, how little help there was for women that wasn't dismissive, commercialized, or a bandaid. She discovered how much power she had inside to heal herself, and knew she had to share what she had learned with as many women as possible. She lives with her daughter, Savannah, her partner, Brandon, and their pets, Denza and Starbuck in British Columbia, Canada.

Website: www.wildwomanmagick.com
Instagram: https://www.instagram.com/wildwomanmagick
Facebook Page: https://www.facebook.com/wildwomban
Facebook group: Run Wild With Her
Email: loverunwild@gmail.com

5

DANIELLE MOORE

MY LIGHT

lashback to 2017: my rock bottom. I thought my life was over. I felt unworthy of being on this earth and wanted to crumble away. In my mind, I was a mental case; I was stuck in a toxic relationship and I was deeply unhappy. I was disappointing all those who were closest to me, and felt horrible for how deeply I had dug myself into a dark hole. I didn't think there was any coming back from how low I was. I didn't think I could ever muster up the courage or strength to turn my life around. I hated everything about myself and who I had become. My depression was eating me alive. Every day I could feel myself growing sadder, crazier, and more unhappy until I reached the point of numbness. This was no way to live, I thought.

Flash forward to 2021. I am a brand new business owner living out my dream as a mother to be, a Mindset Coach for individuals struggling with their mental health, and a girlfriend to the most loving, supportive and grounded man that I get to call my beloved, Cameron. My life is more than I ever could have dreamed of and I am doing what I thought was never possible for myself. So, how did I go from my rock bottom to this? Here is my success story.

For so long, I was limiting myself from growth and expansion without realizing it. Knowing that I was living with depression and anxiety caused me to sulk and wallow in self-pity. I was self-sabotaging my mental health by stigmatizing myself. No one had ever placed mental health stigmas on me, except for me. I was constantly convincing myself that I could never be successful or happy because I had a mental illness, and that people with mental illnesses suffer. I thought.

This limiting belief was my crutch, and I held onto it for dear life because deep down I was scared to do the inner work. I was afraid to face all of the shadows, traumas, and old wounds that had been building up in me for so long. I knew there would be so much to unpack in order to start healing, and I didn't know where I would start. It seemed too hard, and my lower self wanted to stay in her comfortable misery rather than getting uncomfortable in order to grow.

I played with this self-sabotaging behavior for years. After I hit my rock bottom in 2017, when I didn't want to be alive anymore, I decided it was finally time to start taking ownership of my life—for my life—rather than feeling sorry for myself. I needed to get help.

Therapy was my first route towards inner success because it was the first time I was letting somebody into my world—my real world—not the fake smiles and laughs I had become so used to portraying. This was a big deal to me, and was frightening and liberating all in the same breath.

I remember my first session vividly. I went into the session thinking that all of my mental health issues stemmed from the toxic relationship I was once in, so I figured we would address that, and then I'd be good! That was denial (insert sweaty, nervous laughing emoji). Little did I know I had a zillion other root issues that had been tucked away since childhood, so there was actually a hell of a lot more to unpack than I thought. Part of me felt excited that this was the beginning of a long, beautiful journey where I could finally gain some clarity around my life; the other part of me wanted to run from all the tears I knew were coming with each session.

I learned a lot through therapy. I learned what worked for me in my individual healing journey, which I later continued to search for as I sought out coaches, mentors, and healers. There were two components to therapy that were the most profound medicine for me: someone to validate my emotions and someone to hold a nurturing, safe space for me. These key factors continue to be the simplest yet most supportive tools to help me find personal healing, and ultimately a successful life.

Before therapy, I had a tendency to fall victim to the mindset that "other people have it worse, so who am I to complain about my problems," which kept me feeling like my problems were not valid, and I should never express myself. I was always trying to convince myself that I was *fine* and what I was going through "wasn't a big deal." I convinced myself that it was *me* being "oversensitive" or "dramatic". Yet, when my therapist sat there in our first session, after I unloaded what felt like years of trauma, and said "Wow, Danielle, that is *a lot* to go through," I had never felt so validated in my life. I felt like all the problems I brushed under the rug, because I didn't think they were big enough to be talked about, were now worthy and important. Being validated by my therapist that my emotions were worthy opened up the space for me to feel seen and understood. This opening created a sense of self-worth for me. Validation taught me to always speak up, feel my emotions, and hold compassion for myself, becasue regardless of the struggles anyone else is going through, it will never make mine any less valid, worthy, or important.

The second thing my therapist provided was her ability to hold a safe space for me. Now, a lot of us get this confused with venting, but they are not the same. I had been relying on venting to friends which never resulted in feeling the massive shift that I did when I shared things with my therapist. When we are venting to friends, family, or co-workers, without asking if they have the space to hold us, we may not receive the nurturing support we are looking for. This can leave us feeling empty after a "vent sesh". However, when I was able to sit down in my therapist's office for an hour each week, during a time that she dedicated solely to me, I felt safe for that hour. It didn't feel empty like venting did; it felt wholesome and healing because she was fully present, holding zero judgment, while allowing me to speak my truth. Having someone to hold a safe space for me was healing because many of my triggers and traumas stemmed from feeling *unsafe* in my life. Feeling a sense of safety allowed me to step into vulnerability, and through being vulnerable I was able to let someone into my world who could support me. I learned what it was to trust and the sacredness of being a space-holder for others.

Therapy was a magical catapult, shooting me into a version of my better self. The breakthroughs I had in my sessions were incredible. I learned so much about myself and gained clarity around my life, but the real transformation was found in those memorable moments of being validated and nurtured.

For so long, I avoided therapy because I thought it meant something was deeply wrong with me if I had to talk about my "problems" to a professional. For a while I felt the need to sneak to sessions without my parents or friends finding out. I feared going to therapy made me look weak or damaged. But the real success within has come in finding acceptance for who I am and what I need in order to thrive, and if that's therapy, then I choose to celebrate it rather than shame it. Therapy led me to deep acceptance within. When you can be fully honest with yourself and accept every inch of you for all that you are, that is the true definition of success. That is the magic.

After realizing I did well working one on one with someone who understood me and could hold the proper space for me, I continued to seek out more guidance. I felt like therapy had scratched the surface in a beautiful way, but I knew I had more to move through in order to expand. I had this craving for personal development and growth that I could feel bubbling inside of me. So about 6 months later, I invested in a personal coach to help me rise into my higher being. This was *life-changing* and where I felt like my healing journey really took off. Shout out to my coach, Gina Frances; I love you endlessly.

This coaching container brought on similar emotions that therapy did, but amplified. I was working one on one with Gina not only in our weekly sessions, but also in personal development content that she provided me with, ranging from mindset work, self love, breathwork, yoga, journaling, and morning routines, to inner child healing, intention setting, and mindfulness practices. I had never dabbled in any of this work before, and I remember constantly being in shock at how transformational it was. I was creating sustainable change through daily habits and practices that brought me into alignment, while also getting one on one support in our weekly sessions. I was feeling alive for once in my life because I was going through a deep soul awakening through this work.

After four months of working with my coach, I felt like I was in a video game of my life, and had just reached the next level with my highest score yet! I felt so accomplished and truly changed from the depressed and anxious girl I once was. I knew she was still a part of me, but I learned how to support her rather than run from her. I learned how to love her rather than hate her. I learned how to manage my mental health sustainably, rather than letting my emotions build up to the point of explosion or break down. I learned how to take care of myself. I was starting to feel in control of my life, which was a breathtaking feeling.

Having an outlet in the form of accountability, support, mentorship, and guidance is what I have to thank so much of my success for, because I wouldn't have been able to rise out of the dark hole I was in by myself. The thing is, no one should have to do that alone. We *get* to receive support and let people into our lives, because doing everything by ourselves and trying to manage things behind closed doors is suicide. It's the ultimate form of self-sabotage that we think is disguised as strength—but it's actually fear. For me, it was the fear of being judged, being a burden, and being seen differently that caused me to push off asking for help. However, when I finally chose to get uncomfortable in the presence of fear, and step into the discomfort by asking for help, my life changed. The safe spaces I was held in by my therapist, coach, and those I trust, have been my light. I shine not because they taught me how, but because they helped me to finally find the light that was within myself.

For so long I didn't feel worthy of shining because of how low I felt. My depression made me believe that I was incapable, weak, crazy, and co-dependent. My anxiety left me feeling paranoid, fearful, and numb. My mind was constantly in a fighting battle with my body making it impossible for me to even get out of bed every day. I was missing school, classes, work, social events, vacations, and all priorities because I didn't know how to take care of myself. I was confused and I didn't understand my mental illness, so I let it consume me. I placed stigmas on myself which only made me feel worse, and I believed that I could not surmount anything due to my depression and anxiety. I figured success wasn't in the cards for me. I figured people like me struggled, suffered, and could never succeed. *I was wrong.*

I am here to redefine success for those struggling with their mental health, because depression and anxiety shouldn't be a label that you let dictate where you go in this life. Whether you have placed mental health stigmas on yourself, like I did, or you've had them falsely placed on you, know that you are so much more. You are fiercely capable of anything. You are powerful and in control of your life once you step into the driver's seat and stop letting depression and anxiety take the wheel. Know that you *can* reach success beyond the stigmas, and live a limitless life of abundance, authenticity and truth. Will you choose clarity over confusion, courage over fear, expansion over limiting beliefs, and acceptance over shame? I did, and because of it, I'm here to tell you my story today.

My journey has empowered me to be authentically me. It wasn't until I took ownership of my life that I started feeling happier and more confident in who I am. The more consistently I lived in alignment with my truth, the more confident I became because I wasn't pretending anymore. I stopped hiding who I was, bottling things up, faking smiles and laughs, and living in fear. My opportunities are limitless now because I'm honest with myself. I have done the deep, inner work and now wake up every day with vitality because I am crystal clear of who I am.

Success to me isn't materialistic, but internal. It's not checking off societal benchmarks, hitting that promotion, or pleasing your parents by following their planned timeline for you. Success is constantly doing the inner work to grow and evolve. Success is whatever feels good and juicy in your body, no matter what that is. I feel success on a cellular level when I am doing what is in my highest good and alignment. I feel success on a cellular level when I am living my truth and being unapologetically me. Success to me has no timelines, rules, or limits because if you're living *your* truth, you are the only one who can determine what that looks like. Find freedom and expansion when you let go of the external factors and follow your inner compass.

Here is your invitation to take your first step toward a brighter tomorrow. Maybe that looks like therapy, as it did for me. Maybe another space where you feel held. But, determine what feels uncomfortable and scary because that is where the growth needs to happen. Hold compassion for where you're at now, and enjoy the growing pains as you evolve and step into your authentic light. You are so worthy of this success, my love.

ABOUT THE AUTHOR

DANIELLE MOORE

Danielle Moore is a Mindset Coach and creator of the Mindful Magic Mentorship course. She helps individuals struggling with depression and anxiety cultivate a healthier mindset, heal old trauma wounds, and discover authentic happiness. Through overcoming her own mental health struggles, she was inspired to become a mindset coach to help others gain control over their lives and find acceptance for their whole selves. Danielle lives in Massachusetts. She enjoys hikes in New England and trips to the beaches in Florida with her partner, Cameron.

Website: https://www.daniellepaigemoore.com/MMM
Instagram: https://www.instagram.com/daniellepaigemoore
Email: dmoore81596@gmail.com

6

DIANA POULSEN

THE CORE ELEMENTS OF EMBODIED SUCCESS

*T*alking about success used to give me a false feeling of self, like talking about external things that did not matter. During the earlier stage of my career, I believed that success was only about climbing the career ladder and having a stable bank account. Success meant achieving what I thought I wanted.

Then, once I started to transform my conditioned beliefs while walking the path of inner alchemy, I met many spiritually-minded people who focused on detaching themselves from "the materialistic world," so talking about success was not even an option.

Both approaches feel extreme to me now. I believe in the middle way. The definition of success has been distorted, and we need to redefine it. Seeing this duality of views has inspired me to find my definition of success—and talk about it.

I am a visionary, creator, and initiator of a new paradigm on Earth. We live in a great time of the shift in consciousness. More and more people are awakening to their purpose. We need new social systems, new ways of creating business, new ways of managing our resources, new approaches in personal transformation, and new ways of working with energy.

My mission is to inspire people to let go of old ways of thinking, reconnect with their true self, step into their true purpose, embody their success codes, and manifest their highest vision.

MY SHIFT

As a child, I loved the process of creation. We are the creation itself; we continuously co-create with the Source. However, staying strong to my views was not easy, so I adapted to the norms of society.

Back then, I believed that I needed specific achievements to feel successful: the best grades at school, the best programs at the university, a successful career, a stable bank account, an apartment in the city center, and a nice car. I did have all of that, but something felt missing. There is nothing wrong with any or all of these things. It depends on motivation. Do we acquire them to expand our life's purpose? Or are we simply hiding the inner emptiness under social status and external *things*?

I studied the Law of Attraction at an early age. I imagined things, focused on them, took aligned actions, and consistently achieved what I thought I wanted. Now, I call it "manufactured manifestation".

I finished university with top grades and was recruited into an EU organization, but as I searched for something that would fulfill my soul, I started to transition between different jobs and careers. With every new job, I significantly raised my salary, just to leave again and take on another challenge. When I became a team leader in the revenue department, I finally understood how much I loved coaching and training people.

In 2010, I moved to a new country to do my second Master's degree, which led to a new job in a bank. This environment felt so foreign to me that I finally made a shift in my life. I decided to take some time for reflection and take a deep look at my life. I was commuting to my workplace for two hours per day, working in one country while living in the other. I communicated in two foreign languages daily while learning a third one; I won a startup competition and spent evenings building a startup. It may look very well like a success story on some levels, but my true self was suffering.

It became a year of awakening. I received a massive push from the force of higher wisdom to make a shift. I got a new, much more creative position in my favorite city in Denmark, and I started to embrace the flow.

I had more free time and spent some of it walking the famous walking trail to Santiago de Compostela in Spain. I met people living life differently and became inspired. Sometimes, we need to step away from the usual environment to realign with our true selves. I noticed that success was different for each of us, and I also saw the magnetic energy of people who defined their lives and their journeys on their own terms.

Soon after the trip, I went to the magical island of Menorca in Spain and further awakened. This magic island had a special message for me. I met people who inspired me and experienced the deep healing effects of energetic vortexes and nature. I became aware that a higher Source wants to work, guide, and co-create with us, and the only thing we need to do is let go of our old ways.

I quit my job and embarked on a journey of rediscovery to live in alignment with my true self. While visiting different countries and spiritual locations, I experienced a deep process of inner alchemy and purification of old wounds, stories, and conditioned beliefs, while learning from highly evolved teachers.

It is incredible how many conditioned layers of beliefs I discovered, how many patterns and habits had to leave my system, and how many old wounds came to the surface. The process of inner alchemy, transformative relationship, profound methods of personal and spiritual growth, Quantum Flow, Kundalini awakening, and intense purification returned me to the Source. The shift occurred. My life no longer belonged to me; I became a co-creator of the rising collective consciousness.

I stopped seeing "success" as a by-product of my ego desires. I AM A SUCCESS. I co-create with the Source itself. The true definition of success is always individual, authentic, and ever-evolving. The definition of success will depend on the level of one's consciousness, purpose, soul mission, and higher vision.

EMBODYING SUCCESS

We are co-creators of true success. Once we reconnect with our true self, step into our purpose and mission, and actualize our vision while being in service to humanity, we are a success.

It doesn't matter how big or small our mission appears to us; it's part of the great unfolding. It can be raising a healthy-conscious family, becoming a healer, a sustainable architect, an activist driving change, a designer making comfortable clothes, or teaching and coaching people.

I had to drop many other people's ideas to start living life and create my own business from this space. My success formula combines living life from my true self and in a high-energy environment with having healthy relationships, a team, and collaboration partners who support and align with the same business vision. I thrive living my purpose, actualizing my vision, and having enough time to relax, retreat, and visit places of special energetic charge. Letting go of control led me to a deeper level of embodied success. I love co-creating life with the Source.

Aligning with my business vision has been another journey of growth, purification, and inner alchemy. Even though I had prior experience in business development, creating a business from my soul has been much more challenging.

Once we start building a business from the very core of our being, everything becomes more personal, vulnerable, and raw. It has taken time to transition from doing business consultancy, coaching, healing, and teaching yoga to finally stepping into my vision and allowing the Source to work through me. It happened when I finally set a conscious intention to dedicate life to be in service to humanity, raising to the next evolution of consciousness.

I took a few online business courses which merely scratched the surface. On the whole they pitched the idea of distorted business strategies and focused on abundance for one's ego desires. That never felt right to me. I tried following strategies, practices, and methods of other conscious business coaches. However, I realized that did not work for me because it did not come from my true self.

I studied human design, astrology, and other personal development systems, and that's what helped me realize my authentic way of creating business. I'm a visionary, initiator, and connector, and I have adjusted my business template to support that role.

I also learned to connect with the consciousness of the business. When I start a new project, I always tune into its consciousness and see how it wants to work through me.

Another critical aspect of soul success is embodiment. Sometimes we do tend to envision ideas, or visions, but fail to actualize them. When we see that reality does not meet the results, we tend to self-sabotage, procrastinate, and feel bad about ourselves.

But embodiment is the key to bringing our vision to reality. Everything is energy, and so are we. If we are not ready to hold the energetic frequency of our vision, we cannot attract it. It means that we need to work on the emotional, mental, physical, and spiritual embodiment.

It's important to emphasize the resources we need to actualize our vision: time, money, training, inner healing, building a team, forming connections and partnerships, skills in conscious investment, and financial management. Once we co-create with the Source itself, we let go of measuring our worth based on money, and we become a vessel of "surrendered detached manifestation", manifestation from the true self. All the abundance of resources that we receive will support our vision.

ACTUALIZING MY VISION

Bringing the knowledge and skills in team leadership, finance management, embodiment practices, coaching, and subconscious healing methods, I created a foundation for my true business vision that aligned with my true self, purpose, and mission.

In 2017, I founded the Flair Academy that is the embodiment of my vision. It connects services, projects, and people who contribute to visionary business development, conscious finance and investment consultancy, courses in personal transformation, and individual embodiment coaching.

Creating new systems to match the rising consciousness on Earth is a challenging task, and I believe we're so much stronger together. Building the platform for different projects and collaborations has been my long-term vision.

My process of internal alchemy, different training, coaching, and teaching experience has supported me in creating the embodiment coaching program based on the core nature elements. We are nature, and once we balance, purify and refine our elements, we come back to our natural state. Once we start living from this state, sustainable soul success becomes a natural manifestation. Being a teacher of embodiment methods such as Kundalini yoga and Quantum Flow, I know that the body has immense potential for transformation and manifestation.

I called the program "The Core Elements: Follow Your Flow" because I believe that once we tap into the infinite wisdom of our true self and higher vision, everything unfolds naturally without too much controlling, pushing, and struggling. We only need to take soul-aligned actions.

Our old stories, subconscious programming, conditioned beliefs, and inner child wounds stop us from embodying soul success. After working with hundreds of people, I discovered the importance of looking into our relationship patterns. Whether it is a relationship with parents, colleagues, partners, work itself, business, success, or our body, it will all lead to a relationship with ourselves. Once we master our relationship with ourselves, we will master our relationship with success. This awareness and all the powerful tools I have learned through the years is landing into the new self-mastery program "Love Crystal." We are love and success itself.

My work is dedicated to individuals, teams, and groups who want to live their life from their true selves, align with their purpose, transmute their old stories and wounds, and bring their vision to reality while being supported by needed resources.

I am ever-evolving in my purpose and vision in co-creation with the Source, and I trust that the right people will always show up my way. I felt guided to envision and initiate so many beautiful projects, and I am beyond grateful to have my team and my conscious collaboration partners co-create each of them.

Embodied success is a path of inner freedom, outer expansion, and service in creating a bridge between Heaven and Earth.

THE CORE ELEMENTS TO YOUR EMBODIED SUCCESS

I have been training in various embodiment and coaching methods, but I love simplicity. Coming back to the core elements is my way to uncover the secrets of embodied success and following your flow in life.

Foundation of Success. Earth.

Foundations start with grounding. If we want to grow a strong tree, we need strong roots to anchor it. Once you are grounded, you land and accept the reality that you are in right now. Sometimes we rush to act on our visions, not fully seeing where we are and what needs to be transformed. In this way, it's like building a house on ice. Once the ice melts, our house will collapse.

My recommendation is to stop and accept reality as it is. Look at different areas of life, so you are aware of what needs to shift and what you chose to prioritize right now. Once you take inventory of your life, you will know your next step. Awareness is key to change.

It is also essential to cultivate a feeling of gratitude for who you are and where you are right now, so you grow from that place.

It is the time to reflect on our vision and all the obstacles stopping us. Once we become aware, we commit to transforming the challenges.

Healing the Old Stories of Success. Water.

My clients find this stage especially difficult. We haven't been taught about emotions at school and how important it is to feel our feelings, heal inner child wounds, and karmic imprints.

It's the phase when we focus on healing and clearing that which no longer supports us in achieving our vision and embodying our success. It is essential to heal old wounds so that we can become whole from within. Only once we become complete from within will we manifest our authentic soul's success.

The water element reconnects us with love inside ourselves and radical self-worth. This healing process will continue; however, the more we heal, the more aware we are, the more tools we have, the less triggered we will become by external obstacles.

Clear Mindset of Success. Air.

Once we heal our deepest wounds and triggers, our minds will naturally become more peaceful. Once our mind becomes more relaxed, we will start connecting with the nature of the mind, which is luminosity and pure clarity.

Once our minds are peaceful, everything will become more effortless; new ideas will flow, decisions will be made naturally, our creation will happen faster. We will speak our truth with no hesitation and doubt.

Doubts, limiting beliefs, and fears will not be affecting our conscious decisions, and we will always know our next steps towards the actualization of our vision. I teach specific ancient mind-training practices to experience clearer states of mind.

Once we start functioning from the higher mind, it will be easier to adopt a soul-success mindset, and we will feel more confident about our purpose, mission, and the highest vision for our life and business.

Inner Power. Fire.

Once we start functioning from the higher mind, we are ready to ignite the inner fire of transformation and let go of any stored energy blocks. I practice and teach specific embodiment practices such as Quantum Flow, Kundalini yoga, and Mindful Breathing.

The phase of the fire element focuses on the power center where we strengthen our field of intention, so our visions can manifest. I teach my students to do particular practices to embody their vision, release energy blocks and live a life from their true self.

It is a crucial step to embodying your soul's success. Once every cell of your body is vibrating the frequency of your higher vision, you will become a magnet to all the opportunities and resources needed.

You transmute your emotions and thoughts through previous phases, and now they form an electromagnetic field that will attract what you need to bring the vision to reality. The more refined is your energy field, the easier it becomes to move through obstacles.

You tap into the inner power to stay committed and align actions with ease, grace, and flow. It is when the strategies of your business, vision, or project are implemented.

You are a Success. Space.

Once we implement strategies and take actions, we take some time to reflect on the process and rest in the space of success itself.

We haven't been taught at school to "just be", as many of us believe that only doing and acting will bring us the required results.

It is essential to find time to be and bring awareness to what needs to shift or stay. Once we merge into the state of being, we become open to receiving. If we are not available to receive, how can we expect to receive the resources and results in our life?

It is the time to let go, integrate, and open ourselves to the more in-depth wisdom of life and remember that success is co-creation with the Source itself. It's the time to detach from the experience.

Once we reflect and give space to our project to flourish, we can again come back to the cycle of the elements and find inner stability for a renewed vision.

THE SECRETS TO EMBODIED SOUL SUCCESS

What is the embodied soul success?

- It will always be unique and authentic to everyone.
- It will come from an embodiment of your true self.
- It will be aligned with your purpose, mission, and highest vision.
- It will reflect your energetic frequency, the healing process, and inner power to take aligned actions.
- It will ever evolve and grow.
- It will require persistence, determination, and surrender to the highest wisdom.

- It will up-level through stages, levels, and layers.
- It will become a part of you.

Remember, you are SUCCESS.

Tap into the wisdom of your soul, and lay the foundation of practices, methods, and action steps required to embody it here and now.

ABOUT THE AUTHOR

DIANA POULSEN

Diana Poulsen is the founder of The Flair Academy, a Conscious Business Mentor, and an Embodiment Coach. She helps individuals and groups to awaken their purpose, embody their vision, and create sustainable success with ease, grace, and flow. Prior to this, she held roles as an innovation consultant and team leader at various organizations. Following her inner alchemy process, she embarked on her mission to initiate new methods and approaches to business, personal and spiritual growth as the collective consciousness rises to a new level. Diana holds certifications in Transformational Coaching, Mindfulness, Quantum Flow, and other embodiment methods, as well as a Master of Science degree in Innovation Management.

Diana is also the co-founder of Shelab, a transformational women community, co-creator of self-mastery program "The Shift", and a Visionary Business Accelerator. She has facilitated more than 100 inspirational events and workshops and has been featured in several women's magazines and podcasts.

Websites: www.theflaircademy.com
www.dianapoulsen.com
LinkedIn: https://www.linkedin.com/in/diana-poulsen/
Facebook: https://www.facebook.com/TheFlairAcademy
Facebook: https://www.facebook.com/
groups/consciouslivingwithdiana

Instagram: https://www.instagram.com/diana__poulsen/
Pinterest: www.pinterest.com/TheFlairAcademy
dianap@theflairacademy.com

7

DINA BEHRMAN

THE JOURNEY TO INNER SUCCESS

*a*s I sat sipping champagne in the exclusive club surrounded by 'It-girls' and TV stars, trying to make small talk with the woman next to me, a pang of sadness washed over me. From the outside I was successful. I had a flourishing career as a showbiz journalist, working on a popular weekly magazine. I had a life that to most looked fun and exciting; I regularly went to celebrity parties and red carpet events and I met and interviewed well-known stars. On paper, I was a success. But though the job had been fun and exciting to start with, over time it had become gradually less so.

I'd started out as an enthusiastic reporter for my local newspaper. It had been my dream to be a journalist for a long time, so I was over the moon when I landed a junior reporter role. The job gave me an amazing training ground where I learned so much. But soon after, I became hungry for more. A good friend at the paper, Katie, had left and started working for a celebrity magazine and told me, "They need people with newspaper experience to come and do shifts. You should apply!"

So I did. I started doing shifts on the showbiz desk on my days off from the local paper. We had to work weekends and evenings covering local news, so we were given Fridays off regularly in lieu. I booked up my Fridays with magazine shifts; I was eager to get all the work that I could to enable me to eventually be able to leave the local paper and move into working on national publications.

I built up my experience, and after a while, the magazine offered me a longer-term block of shifts to work in their offices, write showbiz news, and interview celebrities and reality TV stars. Writing about celebs for a living had never been something I'd planned for but this was an incredible opportunity and the work was fun. I handed in my notice at the newspaper and started working at the magazine.

Eventually, I took on shifts at other showbiz magazines; once you had that experience there were always other similar magazines who could offer you work. And so, I unexpectedly found myself specializing in showbiz reporting.

After a couple of years, I landed a permanent job on yet another weekly showbiz magazine. After all this time doing blocks of shifts here and there I was grateful to have a permanent job. And when I was offered a regular column alongside two fellow journalists, reporting from celebrity parties and red carpet events, I was thrilled. We were given a professional photo shoot for our party column byline picture. This was it! I was officially being paid to attend celebrity parties.

At first, it was amazing. I attended all these exclusive parties dressed in sparkly frocks borrowed from the fashion cupboard at work, and there was always champagne on tap.

But often I'd have to go to the parties alone as there were no plus ones. And then there was the pressure to get exclusive stories. "So-and-so's going to be there," my editor would say, naming a particular TV star or pop star that the magazine happened to be interested in that week. "Make sure you speak to them!" And I'd find myself practically stalking that particular person, following them all evening in the hope I'd manage to get a few words from them that we could spin into an 'exclusive' story.

There was also a less glamorous side of the job. At one point, I was sent off to a five-star hotel with a wodge of cash in my handbag to interview the father of a famous pop star whom the magazine was paying to tell his story about becoming estranged from his daughter. He ordered the most expensive things on the menu and left me to pick up the tab, and then propositioned me at the end of the interview. Not my finest moment as a journalist.

On top of that, the focus that we were encouraged to give to how female celebrities stay in shape and what they eat felt uncomfortable. Some of the stories the magazine covered felt intrusive especially the unrelenting obsession with reality TV.

Slowly I felt the negative parts of the job starting to outweigh the positives.

Don't get me wrong, I'd had some amazing opportunities that I would never have been able to experience otherwise for which I was truly grateful. I'd been to Ascot, Wimbledon, the Cannes Film Festival, and I'd also made some wonderful fellow journalist friends. And when it had been good, it had been really good.

Until it wasn't. Behind closed doors, my personal life was suffering. When I discovered my long-term live-in boyfriend had been cheating on me, his comeback was: "Well, you're always out all the time!"

Deep down, I knew that my being out several nights a week wasn't the whole story—but it certainly hadn't helped matters.

To top it off, my naturally introverted self found the constant need to make small talk with people at showbiz parties exhausting. Sometimes I'd find myself filled with anxiety at the thought of having to attend yet another event on my own, knowing that I was expected to work the room and return with a story.

I felt conflicted. On the one hand, I knew I was lucky to have all of these opportunities. But on the other hand, there were so many occasions where I found myself at an event, trying to feign enthusiasm, when all I wanted to do was be at home, curled up on the sofa watching TV. I was a 'success', but I realized it wasn't my version of success.

One day, I received an invitation from a charity to go to Zambia for a week with their celebrity ambassador and a couple of other journalists to report on the work the charity was doing there.

That week was life-changing in more ways than one. Meeting and playing with children at schools in the Zambian villages was eye-opening and amazing and humbling all at the same time. It got me thinking about my priorities and what was really important to me. And for the first time in a long time, I was able to really get my teeth into writing an in-depth feature. It also just so happened that one of the other journalists on that trip was working on a newspaper supplement and was looking for a commissioning editor to come and look after their Real Life features section. "You'd be perfect for it!" she told me.

Once back in the UK, I was invited to meet her editor to find out more about the job. I interviewed and was offered the role. I'd be working three days a week in the office, meaning I'd have two weekdays to myself to focus on freelancing.

I started my new job shortly after breaking up with the boyfriend. It really felt like a fresh start. I was in charge of the Real Life section of the magazine and commissioned stories about all kinds of people from all walks of life.

My inbox was constantly inundated with emails from people wanting to be featured but we only had spots for two features a week, so I quickly became very good at spotting a good headline and a newsworthy story angle.

On my days off, I started focusing on writing health features for national newspapers. I loved being able to really dive into learning about a subject, researching it and interviewing case studies and experts.

But after two years in my job, following a round of redundancies, I was told they no longer had any work for me. Initially, I felt a devastated—but I soon realized where one door closes, another door opens. This was my chance to make a full time living as a freelance journalist. It was a bit of a scary proposition, but it was exciting.

At first, I had to get used to being on the other side of the fence; I was the one pitching the editors with the overflowing inboxes and initially this proved to be quite hard. I'd either get the 'thanks, but no thanks' responses or my emails would go completely ignored. I realized I needed to perfect my pitching skills. It took trial and error, but eventually I nailed it and became published in virtually every national UK newspaper and several magazines.

A while later, I decided I needed to diversify with my work. I took a course in copywriting and set myself up as a sole trader, offering PR and copywriting services. After ten years of journalism, I decided to wind down that side of things and focus on running my own business.

Initially I made every rookie mistake in the book: I didn't know who my ideal clients were, I didn't have strong boundaries in place, I took on anyone and everyone who wanted to work with me, and I massively undercharged, meaning I ended up overworked and underpaid. It was a big learning curve.

It was during this time when I met and started dating a lovely man who was supportive of me and my work, no matter what.

A few years passed, and my boyfriend became my husband. When our eldest daughter was born, I took some time out, and when I came back to work I had a renewed sense of purpose. I realized my real passion lay in teaching business owners how to do their own PR. I was ready to stop playing small and get myself out there. I hired a business coach, rebranded and re-launched as a PR coach.

My clients started achieving amazing results. But I still wasn't putting myself out there the way I could have been. If anything, I was hiding. I was suffering from imposter syndrome, and often felt that at any given moment I was going to be found out as a fraud.

When my business coach asked me, "What resource do you have that you're not using?" it hit me: I needed to start practicing what I preach and get visible. I started putting myself out there and truly owning my expertise. I was featured in places like Forbes, Entrepreneur Magazine and HuffPost. And my business took off.

After our second daughter was born a few years later, rather than slowing down, my business sped up. Successful entrepreneurs started hiring me as a publicist to do their PR for them. I had so much work, I had to hire freelance PRs to support me. I was super busy and my clients were being featured all over the place – Forbes, Business Insider, Marie Claire, BBC, Fox News. Doing this work made my heart sing. I was helping these businesswomen share their inspiring stories and expertise in the press, enabling them to share their message with hundreds of thousands of people all over the world. And they were experiencing massive growth in their businesses as a result, often securing thousands of dollars-worth of business after being featured, as well as landing TED talks, magazine columns, radio shows and book deals. One client brought in ten new clients from just one article, another had a successful five-figure launch on the back of an article, another brought in 1500 leads and several high-ticket sales after being featured.

But soon I reflected that again I had created success at a cost. As much as I loved my clients and loved this work, I found myself putting huge pressure on myself to constantly get results for my clients. Juggling work and two young kids, I constantly felt like I wasn't doing enough—and it was exhausting. I felt stretched as a mum and as a business owner, and this often left me feeling like I was failing at both. I'd feel guilty if I wasn't constantly pushing, pushing, pushing and getting my clients results, but then I'd feel guilty for not giving my kids enough attention. I felt like I was heading towards burnout. I knew things had to change.

So I decided to really pare down what I was offering in my business and focus on semi-passive income streams. I created a self-paced course, PR Power, to teach business owners at any stage of business how to do their own PR and I created a PR Mastermind for those higher-level business owners to have my support to get featured, without having to do it all for them. Later, I added an extra service to the mix by publishing multi-author books. Fundamentally, my passion has always been to tell people's stories, or to empower them to tell them. This has never changed.

Eventually, I made the decision to stop taking on any 'Done For You' PR clients. Although this had been by far the most lucrative way for me to make money, I realized my version of success meant being able to support my clients to get fantastic results without feeling under pressure and without it taking all of my time, energy and focus. I wanted to be able to spend time with my kids and not feel like I had to be 'on' all the time. Cutting back to just these core offerings allowed me to do this while still enabling me to have a thriving business, and do work that makes a difference in the world. Finally, I'd found the sweet spot where I wasn't having to run myself ragged trying to do everything myself.

Today, I feel like I finally have reached success, and most importantly, *my* version of success. It's taken me years to figure it out, but I've come to know that success can mean different things at different times in your life—and this can and will change—and that's ok. I've also realized that success on paper is very different to genuine success that fulfills you. Success for me means having a work life and personal life that light me up, having strong boundaries in place, being my own boss, making a positive impact the world and, most of all, doing it all on my terms, in a way that feels light, joyful, and fun.

Success means feeling fulfilled in my work life, doing work that genuinely helps others, while also having plenty of time to spend with my husband, kids, friends and family. Above all, I've learned that feeling successful on the inside is so much more important than looking successful from the outside.

ABOUT THE AUTHOR

DINA BEHRMAN

As a former journalist-turned-PR strategist, Dina Behrman works with entrepreneurs who want to stop being the internet's best kept secret and become the go-to expert in their field. She empowers them to do their own public relations and leverage the media so they can share their story and create a larger impact. She launched her business following a decade working as a journalist, during which she was published in virtually every national UK newspaper and many magazines. She has worked as a publicist for high-net-worth business owners and has enabled hundreds of entrepreneurs to do their own PR. She has been featured as a PR expert in Forbes, Entrepreneur, Huff Post, The Guardian, BBC radio, amongst others. She lives in the UK with her husband, two daughters and cat, Bobble.

Website: www.dinabehrman.com
Instagram: www.instagram.com/dinabehrman
Facebook: www.facebook.com/bizfamecoach
Facebook group: www.facebook.com/groups/businessfamecollective
LinkedIn: www.linkedin.com/in/dinabehrman

8

FRIEDERIKE SADHANA VON BENTEN

FROM STRESS TO SUCCESS: HOW TO GRACEFULLY MASTER CRISES

WHAT I BELIEVED SUCCESS IS ALL ABOUT

*W*hat is your definition of success? Is it making $10,000 a month or more? Is it working with the most influential CEO and thought leaders? Is it being featured in books and magazines? Is it having a prestigious position in a world-famous company?

Or is it having a luxury car (big German label, hello!), a stunning apartment, or other fun toys?

To me, these have been my success measurements until my early thirties.

I grew up in an academic family where everyone around me held a Ph.D.. I soaked up the idea that success for a young woman (or human being of any gender) means to have an academic title, a prestigious position, and making a lot of money on her own.

After graduating from high school, I put over ten years, a lot of effort, and even more energy into achieving these "success goals."

I chased the standard that I believed would make me happy and feel like I belong. I climbed higher and higher in the so-called success ladder. Eventually, I achieved all the above-mentioned "Definitions of Success"—but they came at a high cost.

A LOUD CALL FROM MY SOUL

It is June 2016, a grey and cold day in Germany.

I'm lying on sterile, white sheets, facing an old, grey wall in a cold and impersonal room. The rain is dripping down the large windows to my right.

On my left, I can hear my roommate having difficulties breathing. There are all kinds of tubes coming out of her stomach and her throat.

Without thinking, I'm moving my arm a bit too rapidly, which immediately gives me that icky nauseating reminder that a long IV needle is in my hand with a constant cortisone flow into my veins.

The night before, the young doctor in the emergency department had diagnosed me with tinnitus and loss of hearing. He told me to pack my bag and check in with the hospital immediately.

Now, facing that grey wall, I was all on my own. I had no coworkers and boss around (whom I always tried to impress and please) and no appointments in my calendar (which I believed I'd always attend or else risk the world stopping turning around). I realize that I've been on the wrong track for quite a while.

Three days later.

"The hospital is saying that they will send you to the CT (Computed Tomography) to get some pictures of your head, to see if everything is alright with your brain. But I would rather send you to see a psychotherapist," my family doctor calmly says after I explained to him what has happened.

I start crying. Again, I feel like such a failure. So weak, and not like the strong and successful businesswomen I tried to keep up with all the time.

MY EXPERIMENT OF SURRENDER

Roughly one year later, it's May 17th, 2017, and I'm having a moment of pure ecstasy and joy, jumping and dancing around in my apartment.

"I did it! I did it!!!" I'm shouting in excitement.

"I quit my job!"

I knew very well that the sound in my ear did not come from any physiological issue with my nerves. I did not doubt that instead, it was a loud and clear signal from my soul, telling me: "Girl, watch out. You're on the wrong track! I need to be a little bit drastic here, but otherwise, you literally won't listen to me!"

And no doubt she was right!

I hadn't listened before.

All the silent whispers, all the apparent cues, the voice saying, "This is not the life I want to live! Something is off, and it feels terribly wrong." I ignored them.

At this point, I am so far removed from myself that I started to numb the pain of my soul with binge eating. Just to throw it up again because I feel so guilty. Which prompts a vicious circle of self-reproach, working even harder to prove I am worthy, to feel even more exhausted and a stranger to myself.

I know I'm in trouble.

Luckily, life sends me a precious soul in the form of a new partner, who encourages me to "f*ck everything" and do my own thing!

And I do.

I quit my well-paid and safe job.

I sell my pretty BMW.

I let go of that beautiful apartment at the Yacht port.

I give away all my furniture and belongings, except for a couple of boxes of my favorites.

We purchase a one-way flight to Bali, as I am keen to get to know the digital nomad scene there and find a way to establish myself online.

After my stay in the hospital, Facebook ads would show me constant offers by coaches who worked remotely and would teach their clients to do the same! It sounds like a dream, never having to go through that spinning door in the company building in the morning, working on my goals and projects instead of someone else's.

Life in freedom and on my terms – could that be possible?

We have no detailed plan of staying or what we will do if it doesn't work out. But instead of freaking out about this (which would have been my usual pattern, as a conditioned control freak), I have such a deep trust that everything will work out perfectly fine, and that I will say "Yes" to whatever would show up.

I decide to start my *surrender experiment*[1].

MEDITATION IS KEY

If I'm tracing back the events leading to my stay in hospital and all the drastic changes I made to my life afterward that allowed for this deep trust, there is one big signal post on the way: Transcendental Meditation (TM), which I learned in early 2016.

TM is an evidence-based Meditation, not focusing on breathing or chanting, like other forms of meditation. Instead, it encourages a restful state of mind beyond thinking, the transcended state of mind. You effortlessly go beyond the surface level of your awareness, a state of deep inner silence. Hundreds of independent research studies have found significant increases in calmness, creativity, energy, clarity of mind, and happiness[2].

Imagine you have a deep, unshakeable knowing for what feels aligned – and what doesn't. Your senses are sharp, and you're very aware of what's good for you and what isn't.

And 99% of the time, you can act upon this inner knowledge, and you get the support you need to do so!

You become even more authentic, more aligned with your purpose, and add more value to people's lives, and, therefore, you are more successful in what you do! For me, this meant stopping spending time in shadow careers and accepting mediocrity!

If I could hand you my first success code?

It would be meditation.

SOMETIMES ONLY TIME KNOWS WHAT IS GOOD FOR YOU!

Back to Bali. And I need to be very honest here...it did not work out at all!

After two months of staying on the so-called islands of gods, I found myself on a plane heading back to Frankfurt, Germany.

What a shame!

I felt like the biggest failure in the universe.

The "I'm going to be a digital nomad in Bali" thing had caught a lot of attention in my social network.

And now I had to go back and admit it didn't work out?

What an embarrassment!

But instead of sinking into a deep crisis, I chose to accept the situation and move forward.

From there, I lived in two communes in Denmark and Italy that are all about meditation and self-expression!

After that humbling experience in Bali, I was grateful to scrub the toilets, make the guest beds and peel potatoes, and have a lot of time for my meditations.

Eventually, I ran out of money, and "miraculously" I was offered an opportunity to step into self-employment for an established consulting company that I'd known for many years.

From my first month back in business, I sometimes made four times as much money as I had earned in my previous job, but while enjoying what I did many times more.

In the end, I believe we have no clue what is *really* good for us from our narrow human perspective[3]. Instead, my daily practice is to trust and surrender to the immense wisdom of the unbounded existence —and my soul's consciousness.

And that is my second *success code* for you:

Listen to your soul, that inner voice (e.g., does this decision feel expanded or contracted?)

Trust it is correct (even if it's suggestions or ideas sound ridiculous at first)

And **Act** upon it (just do it, don't wait until your ass gets kicked!).

> *"Clarity comes from engagement, not thought."*
>
> -Marie Forleo

Before you continue to read, I encourage you to ask yourself:

- What is my relation to the soul?

- If I were to know how I can strengthen that connection, what would I do?
- Have there been times in my life where I listened to that inner voice? What happened?
- And have there been times where I ignored it? How did it feel?

It is best if you journal about these questions, not only think about them. You may be surprised what comes up for you!

RESILIENCE – BE LIKE BAMBOO, MY FRIEND

Crises are a part of life.

The question is, how fast do you recover from them?

A crisis is a turning point: It can be a chance, an opportunity for your (personal) growth. From here, it can only get better!

Like they say: You will be the Phoenix rising from the ashes.

Resilience is like your heat protection.

The fire is burning, yes, but you can stand in flames and breathe through it.

People with pronounced resilience can recover faster from a crisis and learn the most valuable lessons, which prepares them better for future challenging events.

They are more aware of their unique talents and strengths. They can handle stress with more ease and experience less anxiety and depression.

The good news is you can learn how to strengthen your resilience at any age.

THERE ARE MANY KEYS TO STRENGTHEN YOUR RESILIENCE

I've picked some of my favorite resilience key factors that I've come across and are helping me to this day to strengthen my "soul's immune system" and apply efficient measurements that allow me to stand through the storm.

I. Choose Your Perception and Acceptance

Before you can change something, you need to accept where you are at THIS moment.

It doesn't make sense to push away unexpected changes, throwbacks, losses, and disappointments into the abyss of your unconsciousness.

Journal:

1) On a scale from 1-10: Where are you at in your life right now? Do you love your life? (1= my life is not good at all; 10 = I have the most amazing life!)

2) From a loving and compassionate point of view: What would you love to change? (e.g., with regards to your body, your mindset, your emotions, and your energy?)

II. Become Self-Responsible

Being self-responsible means you choose to take your destiny into your own hands.

You start to act rapidly towards your goals, and you're able to make quick decisions (because you know you can change them back or work them out).

You become the heroine of your life instead of its victim.

It can be a little uncomfortable to acknowledge the fact that wherever there is a problem in your life, you're also there! Yet, you can always choose how to perceive the situation and take aligned action on it.

You are the alchemist! You can turn those lower frequencies, feelings, experiences into pure gold.

Journal:

What do you want to let go of and *burn* in your life? (e.g., beliefs, circumstances, feelings, behavioral patterns, things you have tolerated but don't want to tolerate anymore?)

III. Own Your Self-Confidence

Instead of focusing on the problems in your life, getting lost in the analysis-paralysis of why something has happened, you turn your attention to the differences that make a difference: Where are the exceptions in your life, where things have worked out? What did YOU do to make this happen?

You become aware of your inherent strengths and gifts, and you're not afraid anymore to use them and show them to the world!

Journal:

1) List at least 20 strengths, passions, and gifts of yours! What do you love doing?

2) What if you were to live your life using those strengths and passions?

3) What would be a good way for you to commit to that which brings you joy and zest and integrate it more into your life?

IV. Build A Supportive Network

According to the first representative long-term study conducted by Emmy Werner starting in the 1950s, having a healthy network or at least one person who loves and supports you is key to building a stronger resilience.

How many times do you withdraw when you feel bad or not good enough, which leaves you alone with that nasty and mean voice in your head?

You do not have to figure it all out on your own!

You'll be surprised about new perspectives and comfort that comes your way once you stick your head out of your "snail-house". And don't forget: Red wine is not a friend.

Journal:

1) Look at your current relationships and network. Who needs to be released because they don't feel aligned anymore?

2) Ask yourself: Who is supporting me wholeheartedly? Who uplifts me when I listen to their podcast or watch them on YouTube? Strengthen your relationship with these people and spent more time with them.

V. Focus on Solutions and Your Goals

I like to compare our brain to Google.

If I search for "Happiness", I get half a billion search results from the search engine.

If I look for "Happiness that lasts", I only get about nine million results.

The same is true for our brain: the more precise I am on what I want and what I am focusing on, the easier it becomes for my nervous system to find ways to exactly get that[4].

"Problem talk creates problems, and solution talk creates solutions." – *Steve de Shazer*

Steve de Shazer, who, together with his colleague, created the Solution Focused Brief Therapy, found that it does not take years to solve problems and be successful in coaching or therapy, but that the level of our attention dramatically determines the outcome of a coaching/ therapy session. They suggest that you bring your attention to solution mindset instead of analyzing the problem in depth.

Focus on the goal or the positive outcome you want to achieve. Then, you take a close look at all the resources you already have to move towards this goal. Lastly, you start looking for incidences in your near past that already point in the desired direction, allowing you to become aware that you have all that it needs already within you[5].

Journal:

1) Suppose you have achieved your goal. What will be different when you reach your goal?

2) Have there been moments recently when you have felt that you have been heading in the right direction? What did you do that made these examples possible?

3) On a scale of 1 to 10 - if 1 represents the point that you do not have any idea what to do to reach the goal, and 10 means that you know precisely - where on that scale are you right now? Can you explain why you are on x and not 1?

4) What can you do in the next couple of days or weeks to head in the desired direction?

CLOSING THE KNOWING-DOING GAP!

It may be that parts of what I've shared so far are well known to you.

But, hand on your heart, in all honesty, do you live up to this knowledge?

Or do you at times, (like many others including myself) experience the knowing-doing gap?

You know exactly what would be good for you, but you won't act upon it?

Here's the thing:

Look around you. Everything you see and experience is a direct reflection of what you're tolerating in your life.

And you can choose, now, not to tolerate it anymore and take aligned action.

FINAL THOUGHTS ON SUCCESS

Don't get me wrong. I'm grateful for my family and ancestors who prompted me to strive for "success" and get an excellent education. I would not want to miss that stamina I inherited from my grandparents and the encouragement from my parents and teachers to reach for more.

Yet, I came across teachers and masters who taught me a different perception of success and what it means to live life to its fullest.

That does not mean that this kind of life is more straightforward! It can be challenging to be true to yourself and to choose the off-beaten track.

However, I believe staying true to your soul and creating an awesome connection with it is a guarantee for your success!

Your soul never fails you.

Communicate with your soul before it sends you strong signals like pain or dis-ease (or a nagging tinnitus).

The answers you get may not be what you want to hear.

But it will become easier over time. It's like a soul gym!

As I finish this chapter, I'm sitting in one of my most beautiful spots in the world. I hear the waves, and I see the mountains across a vast lake. The sun by now is shining warmly on my feet.

There's no way I could have imagined sitting here years or even weeks ago.

But here I am.

Because I listened.

I trusted.

And I took action.

You are success.

You are abundance.

You are the life beyond your wildest dreams.

You are.

And that is the truth of your soul.

---

1. *The Surrender Experiment: My Journey into Life's Perfection*, written by Michael A. Singer is a captivating and motivating book, that illustrated by the author's own life story and how rewarding it can be to say Yes to life and let go of excess of control.
2. Source: https://www.tm.org
3. This is one of the lessons taught in "A Course In Miracles" by Foundation of Inner Peace, which was a big eye opener for me.
4. We can trace this back to our RAS (reticular activating system), a complex neural network that acts as an attention filter. It automatically sorts incoming data (and we know that's a lot in the case of a human brain!) and allows only through what is essential. That's why it is so crucial to be aware of the "filters" you set up!
5. If you want to go deeper, look into Steve De Shazer's book *More Than Miracles: The State of the Art of Solution-Focused Brief Therapy*

ABOUT THE AUTHOR

FRIEDERIKE SADHANA VON BENTEN

Friederike Sadhana von Benten is the founder of Aloha Vita, a licensed psychotherapist, and yoga teacher. She has over ten years of work experience in the corporate world and twenty years studying embodiment techniques.

Sadhana works as a consultant and coach for some of the leading companies in the world. She helps her clients – from admins to CEOs – with a focus on self-leadership, resilience, and mindfulness. Her strongest passion is helping her clients to reconnect with their inner truth, joy, and a feeling of flow and ease.

Sadhana was one of the first certified Quantum Flow Practitioners worldwide. Her greatest joy is to teach this method to groups and individuals to allow rapid shifts in no time. Meditation, nature, and good food are her sources of regeneration.

Website: www.alohavita.com
Facebook: https://www.facebook.com/FriederikevonBenten/
Instagram: https://www.instagram.com/aloha.sadhana/
More on Quantum Flow: https://alohavita.lpages.co/quantumflow
Free gift: https://alohavita.lpages.co/yourfreegift_confidence/
Email: hello@alohavita.com

9

JEANNIE MORAVITS SMITH

SUCCESS: IT'S AN INSIDE JOB. MAXIMIZE YOUR HUMAN POTENTIAL

*S*uccess...what exactly does the word mean? For many, success means reaching a goal, accomplishing a task, or otherwise accomplishing what they set out to do. Essentially, something is a success when the outcome turns out well, is desirable, or is favorable. But beyond that, success is a personal feeling and should be defined any way we want. As we know, beauty is in the eyes of the beholder and, as we have heard, perception is reality. Similarly, success may mean something different to all. Given that everyone is the leader of their own life, we have the choice to define success in a manner that suits our needs and desires. Success influences our motivation and drive, affects our choices and priorities, and is ultimately the basis for all our decisions.

When I was graduating college, I had a vision of what career success was supposed to look like, but when I got there, it was not what I expected. I thought if I climbed the corporate ladder, there would be something amazingly rewarding at the top that I could hang my success hat on. When I made it to the top, there sure was something, but it was no longer something I would have defined as amazing. My perception of success had changed. Or perhaps, *I* was what had changed.

It was only once I had identified my core values, learned my worth, and discovered that which set my soul on fire, that I achieved success. The reality is that I had the same core values my entire life, although I had not yet defined them. I followed the corporate ladder to what I thought would bring me success. I can tell you that I most certainly did know deep down in my soul that the same 8AM-5PM Monday "Good morning, how was your weekend," Friday's "Happy Friday, I hope you have a great weekend," same parking spot, same meet up in the cafeteria, same weekly meetings, same-same-same did not feel right to me. At the time, I continued to follow what I was told would bring me "success"—until I discovered an opportunity to change what I was doing. That is when my *fun* began, when my passion was ignited, and when I really started enjoying "work" and living. Despite what others thought I should do or what they thought success looked like for me, I ventured out on my own to set up HR-Rx, a leadership and organizational development consulting firm founded in 2005.

None of us can achieve success without some help along the way. There are so many people for whom I learned and received help along my career journey. One was not only my financial advisor and a friend, but also very much a father figure to me when my dad was killed by a drunk driver. Joey inspired me to reach for the stars in business, more so than anyone else. He and I would meet regularly, and he was always delighted to hear of my wins. He taught me how to set up a business and educated me on who needed to be on my team to not only succeed, but to thrive long term. He was a phenomenally successful businessman and yet respected me as a strong and influential businesswoman. Sadly, Joey's life abruptly ended in 2014 from an untimely accident. I share this with you as I hope everyone has a "Joey", even if only for a short period of time: someone who shares their wins and helps them define and achieve success. I often play this role for my clients. I share my personal experiences, business knowledge, and leadership skills with others in the hopes of inspiring them to soar to the heights of what they define as success.

With the support of my "Joey", I felt I was already achieving success. When I founded HR-Rx, I had a vision to be a partnered resource to as many leaders as I could. I wanted to make their personal and professional lives easier by outsourcing the human resources aspects of their business to my company and trusting me as a reliable personal and professional coach. For decades, my clients have known their outsourced efforts are managed with the utmost professionalism and confidentiality, and that they can rely on me to be a solid business partner that takes care of all human-centric aspects of the business.

Now at Dynamism Leadership, formerly HR-Rx, we help leaders lead in a manner where a sense of belonging is felt by *all*. We evaluate personal and professional energy, create action plans, and help leaders and their staff embrace change. Our purpose was and is to partner with leaders to flip the switch on the thoughts and feelings controlling their mind so they can live connected to themselves and others, both personally and professionally. Productivity, energy, accountability, and engagement of a business improve when humans are connected. And the business of people has so many facets. I help leaders understand human dynamics and prepare for the unknown. I always come away inspired by those who let me help them reach their next level of success. The core values I hold myself and my company accountable for are integrity, equality, kindness, compassion, trust, and authenticity. Today, these core values continue to shape our leadership coaching and consulting efforts year after year.

True success comes from within—or at least that is where I have found it, in myself and others. Over the course of my career, I have worked with thousands of leaders and have come to realize that success is an inside job. In my experience, many of the people who are viewed as extremely successful are not actually happy or fulfilled in their relationship with themselves, until they have found success in their heart and soul. They only dream of having passion for what they do, and therefore always live feeling there is more for them.

Over the years, I have come to believe that there are certain things that make or break a leader's success. As everyone is the leader of their own life, this applies universally. The five aspects of my success code are: remain open to change, trust and be trusted, be able to confidently communicate, be authentically resilient, and maintain a high level of emotional intelligence. Let us explore each.

CHANGE

Openness to change refers to an individual's level of acceptance and conscious awareness of the possibility that change may be needed across a range of situations and scenarios. I learned early in life that change is inevitable, and when we flip our perspective to see changes as growth opportunities, change is welcomed. For example, focus on believing that things happen *for* you—not *to* you—and always take a moment to ask yourself, "Can I look at this another way?"

TRUST

I have always believed that trust is the number one principle in all successful relationships, including the relationship we have with ourselves. Without trust, true connection cannot exist. When there is a lack of connection, even the best intentions will be wasted. Believe in positive intent, trust others, and show up in a manner to be trusted. Every relationship we have, especially the one we have with ourselves, performs better when led by trust. Live our values in relationships with colleagues, clients, and friends based on integrity. Without integrity, we might as well function solo.

I believe that we all need others to be successful. A solo mission is not only boring but lonely. The best way we build trust is to learn to be okay with others bringing bad news to your attention and learning how to respond versus react when you are surprised by the news. I would encourage everyone to not be afraid to always be honest, even if it is inconvenient. Nothing destroys trust as much as dishonesty. Rather than tell someone what we think they want to hear, tell them the truth. There is always a way to communicate news, whether good or bad. Being the youngest of six children and spending three successful decades in my human-centric career, I naturally hold conversations in confidence, and I do not waste my time with gossip or politics—and know that many of the people I believe are extremely successful do the same. The successful people I know publicly encourage suggestions from others and listen to the contributions with equal respect. The benefit of doing so not only demonstrates that everyone has value to contribute, but surfaces a diverse set of viewpoints, perspectives, solutions, and trust to become stronger as a unit.

COMMUNICATE

Successful leaders must be able to communicate confidently and effectively with themselves and others. Communicating with confidence is an important life skill. Being assertive in conversations with others helps us get what we want and need while standing up for ourselves and our values. Having confidence in ourselves when speaking and writing helps us effectively convey our messages and helps our audience receive our messages in a more meaningful way. Projecting confidence in our ideas helps others to pay attention. Confidence allows us to speak concisely and with clarity. Professionals who communicate with confidence can convey what they want and need in a clear and efficient manager. Effective communication is critically important for career advancement, if that is what we want, and personal success. When we live the values and messages we embrace, walk our talk, share our good news and bad, and, importantly, admit when we have made a mistake, we will succeed.

Communicating confidently also applies to the dialogue you have with yourself. Self-talk is the internal dialogue our own minds come up with. It is influenced by our subconscious mind, and it reveals our thoughts, beliefs, questions, and ideas. Self-talk can be both negative and positive. It can be encouraging, and it can be distressing. Much of our self-talk depends on our personality. If we are an optimist, glass half-full type of person, our self-talk may be more hopeful, uplifting, and positive, also known as anabolic. The opposite is generally true if we tend to be a pessimist, glass half-empty type where catabolic thoughts rule our world. Yet, positive thinking and optimism can be effective stress management tools. Having a positive outlook on life has much to do with our personal measure of success and a greater level of life satisfaction in support of personal success levels. Learning to shift our inner dialogue can help us be more positive and improve our level of perceived success.

Of course, we would be remiss in a conversation about communication without *listening*—*both* listening to hear others and listening to our intuition. We have two ears and one mouth for a reason. We should all practice listening two times as much as we talk. Studies show that we cannot truly listen when we are doing the talking. And this includes our intuition! I have learned that our gut, our deep-down gut feelings we get, will never let us down. When we believe in ourselves and others, we set everyone up with their full potential for success.

BE RESILIENT

Resilience is a function of our authenticity and attitude. When individuals have a high level of authentic resilience, they have proven to exhibit some of the most remarkable feats in short periods of time allowing for successful outcomes. It is okay to be *you* and to show up in a manner that you are most comfortable with. The people who do not 'get' you will not 'get' you—and that is okay. There are plenty of people who will, and they will resonate with what you have to offer.

Our ability to thrive and be successful depends on our resilience and the choices we make.

EMOTIONAL INTELLIGENCE

Emotional intelligence is the ability to identify our own emotions and those of others, to self-motivate and regulate, and to know how to monitor our emotions and those of the people around us.

Individuals with high emotional intelligence are not afraid of change or taking risks, they possess a high degree of self-awareness, they know what they are good at, and do not let their weaknesses hold them back. They can relate to others, ask questions, and are keen to explore possibilities and another's perspective while not placing judgment. They tend to be those who maintain a glass half-full mentality, can create, and maintain healthy relationships, and feel good about their own life.

It is important for anyone setting themselves up for success to create an environment in support of their best performance. Regardless of what it is, we should set ourselves and others up for maximizing human potential. Be empathic and sensitive about what matters most to you and others. Since everyone is different, be mindful to embrace what makes us different and strategically leverage our differences to create and sustain opportunities for ourselves and others.

We will succeed at everything we set our mind to do when we:

- Remain open to change.
- Trust others and show up in a manner to be trusted.
- Communicate with others confidently and effectively and to our self through self-talk and listening to our intuition.
- Are authentically resilient.
- Maintain a high level of emotional intelligence.

My motivation to "succeed" comes from the way I was raised. My mother taught me to never give up on my dreams. Things will change over the years, but when we are passionate about something, giving up is not an option. My drive is sustained when I stop, take a breath followed by a break, then get my head back in the game. I know that tomorrow is a new day and if I am gifted the opportunity to live another day, I always wake up ready to take on all challenges through the eyes of opportunity. It is okay to create success in small and large achievements daily. I often tell my friends, family members, clients, and often complete strangers, "all we have to focus on is one moment of one day at a time". When we chuck responsibilities into manageable pieces anything is possible, and everything is achievable when we set our mind to it.

Much of this is well captured by one of my favorite success related quotes:

> "Who has lived well, laughed often, and loved much; who has gained the respect of intelligent men [people] and the love of children; who has filled his [their] niche and accomplished his [their] task; who leaves the world better than he [they] found it, whether by an improved poppy, a perfect poem, or a rescued soul; who never lacked appreciation of earth's beauty or failed to express it. Who looked for the best in others and gave the best he [they] had."

-Ralph Waldo Emerson

As you read, I hope opportunities that set your soul on fire and things that you are passionate about come to mind, and that you feel able to embrace those feelings you get when you do something that makes you want to jump out of bed each day. You should do the exciting and amazing things that set your soul on fire. We are born on a date and pass away on a date, the dash in-between in yours to create. Tomorrow is promised to nobody, so today is the day for you to take one step closer to your success.

Ultimately, everyone wants to feel that they are adding value to everything they do and having a positive impact on others. Know that if it does not feel good to you, it is not good. If it does not feel right to you, it is not right. If you feel deep down in your heart that there is more for you, there is more for you., And, when you decide to follow your dreams, there is no such thing as failure; these are only learning opportunities getting you closer to achieving *your* dreams, maximizing your human potential, and having success as you define it.

CHEERS TO YOU AND YOUR SUCCESS!

ABOUT THE AUTHOR
JEANNIE MORAVITS SMITH

Jeannie Moravits Smith, Chief Energy Officer, creates breakthrough experiences from the inside out, allowing her clients to create an extremely healthy relationship with themselves and others.

Jeannie is the founder of DYNAMISM Leadership, formerly HR-Rx, a coaching and consulting firm established in 2005. Jeannie has helped thousands of leaders learn how to take charge of the catabolic thoughts and feelings that control their mind and how to use anabolic energy to act and embrace change. Prior to establishing her own firm, she held executive leadership roles at a variety of organizations. Jeannie holds certifications in leadership coaching, energy leadership, & human management, as well as a Master of Science degree in Human Resources.

Fulfilling her passion to help individuals and teams maximize their human potential, Jeannie has taken the stage to share her decades of experience, knowledge, and skills. She is highly regarded for her inspirational speaking ability. She is the developer of several sought-after coaching and training programs and is featured regularly on podcasts, TV shows, and other media outlets.

Website: https://www.DynamismLeadership.com
Instagram: https://www.instagram.com/jeanniesmith777/
LinkedIn: https://www.linkedin.com/in/jeanniemoravitssmith/
Facebook: https://www.facebook.com/DynamismLeadership

Facebook Group: https://www.facebook.com/groups/343240692860566
YouTube:
https://www.youtube.com/channel/UCDwevrcZW6ESJVxl0h3O7xA
Email: info@dynamismleadership.com
Sociatap: https://sociatap.com/JeannieSmithHRRx

10

JESSICA HOEPER, MSW/LISW

SUCCESS IS COLLECTIVE.

*I*magine you are a newborn; you would not live if another person doesn't take responsibility to nurture your growth and development. At its most primal level, this is the collective nature of success.

Now, imagine you are a toddler and learning to walk. Your caregiver starts by holding both of your hands until you have a bit of success. Then they go to holding one of your hands, to not holding your hands at all, yet helping if you fall. Even when they let go of your hands, they are collectively invested in your success.

Now imagine, you are an adolescent, you have a bigger body, and you are seen as more of an adult than a child. Are others still collectively invested in your success? Some will say yes and some will say no. At this stage, success support becomes a privilege. We are given success support from available caregivers, whether this is at school, home, work, extended family, church, community connections, etc. Consider the ways success at this point in development is pushed towards being defined as an independent characteristic. Think of sports, tests, grades, and other standard measures. These are important at their root because we designed them to systematically create healthy competition and measure general ability to learn. But the missing link remains the collective response to "failure".

Currently, the generally accepted definition of success separates success by "winning", without much consideration given to the unintended consequences this may have on collective well-being in the long run. It separates people into an "us versus them" mentality. This is not meant to harshly knock-on sports—I have five children and a husband who love sports—and I in turn do love the opportunity sports can offer in regards to building the collective. Coaches have the role of building a collective desire within their teams, however attention needs to be paid equally to building a collective support response to those outside the team. Cue competition. Competition can give space for practicing success in failure alongside the success of winning. We all need to be able to fail, because we will all be afforded opportunities in this life that will present, at least initially, as "failure". To me, it is no surprise that the word "*coach*", long used in sports, is now widely professionally used to describe career coaching, executive coaching, reflective coaching, and so on. The feeling evoked by the word "coach" is support and connection; something we all need when leaning into failure, celebrating wins, and moving towards our own version of success. A coach helps you to get to know your own skills and areas of future growth.

I often wonder if self-reliance skills are being confused with competition during the adolescent years. Self-reliance is a skill that we want humans to have, but we forget that self-reliant abilities are not universal as we all have differing abilities. And yet, those who are the most independent and self-reliant are praised as most successful, and it is because they "beat out" others to get there. If we really thought about how success comes about, no one can earn it individually.

Now, picture yourself as an adult, and you're going to bed. When you wake up, have you ever thought "I don't want to be successful today?"

No, never. So, you can safely assume that no other adult goes to sleep and wakes up in the morning hoping to be unsuccessful. In fact, collectively we all hope to be successful. Even when mental wellness is low or clinical depression is present, no one wakes up hoping to be unsuccessful. Lack of success is not due to lack of desire for success. If we change the narrative, we give greater access to many more people. The privilege of success is currently set up by the majority definition of success.

Of course, painting a picture of the inequity that riddles our most popular definitions of success may prickle, but it is meant to make you feel stirred, curious and connected!

We are *always* worthy of success and the support needed to get there, and should work to find our own purpose in helping others achieve their unique version of success. Your intuition is always with you guiding you along your unique path of success; now it is time to choose whether to listen to it.

I have worked in the field of human services—specifically child welfare—for over fifteen years. Outside of work, my husband and I are raising five children. I love learning about development and seeing it in action. I have worked with many children and families who are tireless in their pursuit of "success", but are often pushing towards someone else's version of success as a result of not having had the opportunity to define it for themselves. I have, over time, shifted from working *within* the system to working *with* the system as a consultant/coach to offer reflective coaching. My mission is to spread HOPE in the world and hope to me is active, and for HOPE to be active you have to strive to **Help Other People Everyday!** The way I know how to best spread hope is to curate curiosity, within myself and others. I want to help people use curiosity over judgment. I stand for *active* hope: loving others well, living, and being in the moment, while cultivating eagerness for the moments to come.

Success is collective and accessible if we are the definers of it. What I know well is reflection and I love it. I use reflections to guide, encourage, and support collective learning, unlearning, and relearning. Let's reflect on our own narratives around success. Let's dive deep into reflection around success while we are together in these pages! Grab a journal or notebook to harvest your reflections.

Reflection is a form of awareness building. I like to use what I call the Reflective Coaching Path (RCP). The Reflective Coaching Path is an infinite path that follows a cycle along an infinity symbol: it starts with reflection, moves to connection, then into considering, and finally on to nurturing before returning back to reflection again. When we are given a general reflection, we start by naming what we are reflecting on. *(Reflect.)* We are connecting our dots, while looking at themes that are linked to the reflection. *(Connect.)* We then consider, this is where much reflection time is spent in "wonder"; here is the magical juicy part of reflection that includes the curating of curiosity! Get curious about the dots you connected, themes you see, and everything else you find internally that is deeply linked to the initial reflection. *(Consider.)* We wrap up our reflection with nurturing; nurture yourself by choosing new ways/ideas or nurture yourself in finding a deeper connection to the concept reflected on. *(Nurture.)* We will use this path through all the reflective opportunities offered next and on my website.

REFLECTION 1:

When you tune into your intuition, what do you know your "why" for living to be?

Reflect. Connect. Consider. Nurture.

Success is collective. But to participate in the collective experience you need to first be clear on who you are. If you are not deeply linked to why you are on this earthbound journey, then someone else's journey can look like competition instead of uniquely their journey.

For me, working with children and families in need was not something I thought I wanted to do as a career, but it is the place I landed and found my soul's work. I had always known my deep "why" for living was to be connected to others and to walk through the tough parts of life with people. Get deeply connected or reconnected to your why for living!

REFLECTION 2:

What is your current definition of success?

Reflect. Connect. Consider. Nurture.

For a long time, my definition of success was based on acquiring material things. To do this, you must make as much money as you are capable of making and work hard, to the point of exhaustion or to the point of lacking life balance, to reach the ability to earn material things. Success originally looked like the *biggest*, the *best*, and the *most*. This never felt quite right and never felt like it supported others well or equally.

Today, my definition is based on feeling supportive and supported. Supportive in the ways I know deep in my being I am meant to live and love others, and supported by being loved well by others. My current definition of success is sometimes different than what others want for me—my husband and I even have different views of success —but we have found (or, I should say, are finding) ways to honor each other's self-made definitions.

You have to understand your own definitions of success and deeply internalize them as yours, so you can see another's definition with grace and understanding.

REFLECTION 3:

How was your current definition of success built? Who participated in building it?

Reflect. Connect. Consider. Nurture.

My current definition was built over time by many influences and experiences.

All of our successes are built on the support of others. From your entrance into this earthbound journey all the way to today, right now. Consider those that supported your success long before you can remember, like daycare providers so your parents could work, your parent who chose to stay home with you, your extended family, and your teachers.

We are not conditioned to strive for collective success, but at its root it is only collectively achieved. Who gave you your first job, who cared about you, and who gave you your first failure? If someone didn't say you had failed, how would you have known? We collectively define the independent conditions of success, all while never realizing true success will only be felt when connected to the collective!

Notice the collective nature of your success even upon short reflection.

REFLECTION 4:

Consider if your current definition was built by you or for you?

Reflect. Connect. Consider. Nurture.

I was taught and told that success was earned and material-based. I learned to believe that only some were worthy of success and that it might not be me. I wouldn't be worthy because I did not fit the mold of "general", although I tried very tirelessly to fit this mold for many years! I learned that dreams always required a backup plan, especially if your dreams didn't fit into a generally accepted category.

Money was also a success indicator that was built *for* me and not *by* me. Money matters on this earthbound journey, and you can say yes to money, but in my definition it cannot be made at the detriment of another if it is to equal or be a part of your success. The money earned karmically needs to be a window in which others find success too.

I know the moment success being collective shifted for me, and it was not because anyone stopped supporting my success, but because I believed success as I knew it was no longer as accessible to me. And I would also realize that my learned version of success was not available to many, and the reasons behind the "why not" shockingly made more sense. What I had once seen as personal failures, I now saw personal struggles. No one wakes up and wants to fail or be unsuccessful. And yet, here we are, still labeling others as unsuccessful or successful without any knowledge of how they define it for themselves.

REFLECTION 5:

Does your current definition of success make you feel joy and connected to the collective?

Reflect. Connect. Consider. Nurture.

To actively consider this, reflect on the top three things that bring you happiness. Reflect on the top three things that make you feel joy. Are these interwoven into your current definition of success? If not, you are operating within someone else's definition, and it's time to make your own.

REFLECTION 6:

When you reach a review point in your life, will your current definition of success have supported your intuitive "why" for living? (Refer back to reflection 1)

Reflect. Connect. Consider. Nurture.

Upon review of my life, I want to confidently and joyfully say that my lived version of success was dual-purposed and active along an infinity symbol. Success can be dual purposed in that we can be successful while supporting collective success. Don't feel guilty about being successful. Revel in your own success but reflect often, ensuring the successes you are reveling in are strong foundations for the overall success you seek. Notice others and help them along the way to build definitions of success that include happiness, joy, rest, play, and purpose. This can have great impact on generations to come, when the definition of success is collectively linked to displaying our unique gifts instead of competing for the biggest, best, and most. When we see success as a renewable, sustainable resource available to all, we will have achieved a meaningful success definition for the collective!

REFLECTION 7:

Do you want to keep your current definition or rewrite it?

Reflect. Connect. Consider. Nurture.

Concepts in general evolve. This is evident within the human race, but it takes brave souls to start the path of evolving. Think of how years ago, we collectively believed the world was flat. Think of the collective power we can harness in regards to success if we shift our thinking as a whole.

When I reflected on these same questions I have posed to you, over time I have realized that my definition was not built on the things that brought me joy or felt most aligned with what I know to be my purpose in this world. So, I rewrote it. And continue to rewrite it as I actively participate in the world.

If we want others to consider writing their own definitions of success and then living them, we must do the same. It is going to take brave souls to rewrite what has been built over time. But here you are among these pages. Brave Soul, I see you!

FINAL REFLECTION 8:

What is your success definition for others? How do you ask another about their success?

Reflect. Connect. Consider. Nurture.

How often do we ask someone, "What do you do?" to define them by what career they have chosen? We use this as our default to connect and check in on their success? But what if we asked, "How are you living out your soul's intended journey?" or, "How are you finding joy and living that joy?" I am just as guilty as anyone for asking that first question, but when we really think about why we ask that, it is usually because we care about others being well in life, but are just using an antiquated version of how to check in on that with each other!

If we believe success is in fact collective, then we have to quit shaming "unsuccessful" and wonder with curiosity what the barrier to success is in order to *help* others find *their* success. We have to also consider that maybe, just maybe, our success definition is not their success definition and allow the other to tell us what their success definition is! Their personal success deeply matters to our success as a collective.

SUCCEEDING COLLECTIVELY

Real success is not a limited resource! We are not in competition. We all have access to it, if we define it for ourselves. We judge those we deem to be "unsuccessful" so we don't have to equate ourselves with "them". We assume their "lack of success" is because "they" didn't try hard enough, but more likely we landed on this assumption to avoid connection with "them". But once we value our differences, we no longer need to compete.

When you find ways to be authentically you, that is success—and the simple act of just being you should be celebrated over and over. If ever you are feeling prickled or low regarding success, consider reflecting on:

1. "Who defined this for me and does this definition fit or is it time to change it?"

2. "Am I living authentically? How come and why?"

3. "Is there something in my life out of alignment with my definition of success?"

For me I learned that I was happier and healthier when I found my way to my own definition of success. I know that I don't want to gain worldly things and lose what matters most to my definition of success: love and connection.

After reflection comes wonder. Through my work with human service professionals, I curate curiosity using the "wondering why". I often wonder about words. Success. Successes. Successful. Small successes are big steps. Success FULL is broken down into starting with a single success, which turn into many successes, which leads to successful (*success+full*).

If your success has been built through helping others, and I mean really helping others, then your success is collective! Your ripples matter. That is success.

Success is collective!

My success is wrapped up in your success, and yours in mine, so let's be successFULL together!

With Love,
Jess

ABOUT THE AUTHOR

JESSICA HOEPER, MSW/LISW

Jess Hoeper is a licensed independent social worker and the founder of Ray of HOPE, LLC where she provides reflective coaching. As the "helpers' helper", her reflective coaching enhances human service professionals' abilities to serve with curiosity and unconditional love. She is actively driven by HOPE: Helping Other People Everyday. Jess lives in Minnesota with her husband and their five children (yes, you read that right...five kids!).

Website: www.rayofhopereflectivecoaching.com
Instagram: https://www.instagram.com/reflective_coaching/
Facebook: https://www.facebook.com/jrhoeper
Linkedin: https://www.linkedin.com/in/jessica-hoeper-3ba8aba7/

11

JOCELYN CHONG

VASTNESS OF SUCCESS

I'm free and I feel successful with a deep sense of joy running through my veins after quitting my job in exactly the way I had imagined it. My vision of myself leaving corporate with ease finally came true.

I too have seen the vastness of the ocean.

I'm so delighted to embark on my entrepreneurial journey, I feel so certain that my future is bright, successful and promising. I get to choose how I want to run my business on my own terms, and make decisions that are in full alignment with my values and beliefs system. Above all, I'm serving human beings who I love, transforming lives through coaching, and helping my clients serve their dream clients and make money.

I pinch myself every day—I am living my best life right now.

But this is a very different picture than yesterday. Over the last twenty years, I worked in the banking and finance industry achieving at least, *my old definition of success*, winning multiple awards in recognition of my contribution to the company and attending the best of the best conferences.

Everyone defines the word "success" differently.

To me, I associated success with climbing the corporate ladder, being recognised as the best of the best in my field. Gaining a higher status in the society and making multiple six figures was how I perceived myself to be a successful individual.

However, along the way, my sense of identity was heavily tied to my career, and I neglected other areas of my life that were equally as important towards a successful life.

Deep inside, I would feel doubtful, frustrated, resentful and guilty about events occurring in my life.

I would struggle to speak my truth because I didn't want to be judged by others.

I didn't have enough self-confidence to stand up for my own beliefs and values.

There was a voice in my head reminding me I was not good enough, and that I need external validation to feel enough and feel accepted. I also felt insecure about my appearance because I didn't fit into society's norm; I'm not tall, trim, and terrific!

But all these thoughts stemmed from an accumulation of stories that I held from what others said about me, either directly or indirectly in my life. Over time, I embraced them as my own beliefs and values.

SHAPED BY CULTURE

I grew up in a middle-class family in Malaysia. There, I was heavily influenced by my maternal grandmother's standards of success. It was ingrained in my upbringing that, to be successful, I must complete a useful degree so I can land a stable job, then get married to a decent man and build a family!

I was raised to behave perfectly all the time.

Failure is not accepted by my family. In fact, it's taboo to fail. Although deep down her intentions were pure, my grandmother set such a high standard of perfection that it was hard to meet her expectations. And I had real-life examples of success around me who had met these standards; Aunt Jenny was a high-achiever working in accounting, and my role model growing up. I saw her living a life full of glamor and achievements.

When I sat for my National Exam at the end of secondary education, I did not score all A's. I felt like a total failure. I had let down the family and had not achieved success.

Then I entered university, and promptly failed my accounting paper. I felt terrible that my parents had to fork over more of their savings so I could repeat the paper the following year. I sat with nervousness and fear before telling my parents. It took me time to muster up the courage to let them know.

After speed bumps like these, you can imagine how relieved I was when I graduated with a double major in accounting and finance.

Finally, I could make my family proud of this achievement and earn their tick of approval!

After I completed my degree, I was determined to stay back in Australia. Initially, my parents were not supportive of my decision until I persuaded them on the basis that I could support my own living expenses.

When I received the phone call that I was offered a graduate position with a "big 4" accounting firm, I felt another sense of achievement that my career is heading in the right direction—another tick of approval.

It was very glamorous to work for a global multinational accounting firm. I was full of pride because I'd been successful in emulating my aunt's success path as an accountant.

I was finding "success" with my love life too. I was dating a cardiologist and he proposed to me within two years. I couldn't believe that I was fulfilling all of my grandmother's dreams. But, after three months of engagement, he broke it off. I wasn't his perfect match, and he wanted to marry a medical professional.

Feeling crushed, I cried myself to sleep for weeks. I was so embarrassed by this event. It took me years to heal and let go of this painful experience completely.

CLIMBING THE CORPORATE LADDER

So, I decided to devote all my energy to pursue my career. I worked very hard and I was quickly promoted to senior positions. At work I was recognised for my hard work and received many awards. I was earning a good income and began to tie my self-worth and self-identity to titles and achievements.

I felt so important to be assigned to high level interstate projects regularly. I would wake up at 4.30AM to catch the first flight out and I would arrive home at 9PM. Yet after a few years, I began to feel this kind of lifestyle wasn't so classy anymore.

I never saw the daylight. I practically lived in the office or on the plane traveling for work. I didn't have many friends outside of my colleagues, because I didn't have the time to develop genuine friendships. That was an unhealthy work life balance.

Fast forward twenty years, I reflect on my corporate life and how I lived my life. It was not how I imagined it to be. Working seventy hours a week was in fact not glamorous at all.

TURNING POINT

It was a cold winter's morning when I was about to walk into a client meeting. My personal mobile rang several times from my sister. It was unusual for her to ring me at that time of the day, so I thought I'd better return her call.

It was the phone call nobody should receive.

My cousin's wife took her own life the night before. She died at the scene. Tears streamed down my cheeks. She died too young; at thirty-five, leaving behind a baby girl only fifteen months old.

While her husband, sisters and friends were reading her eulogy at the funeral, it dawned on me that life is so short that all the memories can be compressed and shared in less than ninety minutes.

Then, I imagined how I wanted my life to be remembered.

"What would they say about me at my funeral?"

"What kind of legacy do I want to leave behind?"

I wanted to leave behind a legacy that is eternal, infinite and limitless.

Honestly, I was under the illusion that I was living my best life, but I wasn't. I was hiding my own truth.

If my life was a movie, screening my life then versus the purposeful way I wanted to live it would show a huge misalignment on the big screen. My values, beliefs and actions were not congruent.

Determined to change the way I live my life, I embarked on a self-discovery journey.

I started to read more self-help books, listen to podcasts, and attend conferences that were non-work-related.

Change happens when you allow yourself to do so. I gave myself the permission to experience a new level of success outside of work.

I decided that my success is not going to be benchmarked against someone else's standards. But it took me time to realize that success is an inside job. I spent years releasing old patterns and limiting beliefs and adopting a new definition of success. Yet, over time, I developed the self-confidence to no longer need someone else's approval and acceptance to feel successful.

HEALING JOURNEY

At the start of 2020, I was determined to actively work through my limiting beliefs and values I had clung to for many years. I engaged a Spiritual Coach to address areas that I was aware of—and some I was unaware of—that became a barrier for me to progress and live a purposeful life.

As I practiced journaling to deepen my self-awareness and meditation to manage my anxiety and stress, I developed a healthy sense of self-worth, identity shift, and the confidence to live in total surrender and abundance.

As I dug deeper to the way I perceive and judge any situation, I realized I needed to heal my inner child.

Everyone has an inner child. It's a direct representation of yourself in your early years. Through that awareness of my inner child, it has helped me think back to my lighter, carefree years of the joys of my childhood.

Growing up, I didn't associate my childhood with playfulness and fun. I experienced neglect and other emotional pain as a result of illness. I felt small, vulnerable, and in need of protection.

And I had buried these and protected myself so that both my present self and the child were in pain. This pain often re-surfaces in my adult life, showing up as distress in personal relationships.

Healing my inner child wounds came by way of the Emotional Freedom Technique (EFT). With the guidance of my Spiritual Coach, I started to connect with my inner child and listen to her feelings: insecurity, guilt, shame, rejection and anxiety. I traced back all those specific childhood events, and I realised similar situations in my adult life were triggering the same responses. By exploring the past, dealing with the emotional pain from those events, and letting myself experience the feelings, I began to make sense of my reactions.

It was very liberating to heal those wounds. I became more aware of who I am and it enables me to keep working on it to become a better version of myself every day.

REDEFINING SUCCESS

I have a new definition of success. That it is ever changing and without boundaries; not a set marker in the sand but rather the ocean.

It is important to build a business doing something you love. Reflecting on my twenty years in a corporate career, I explored different types of roles and leadership models. Throughout that journey, I realised that I lit up every time I coached someone. Either in a 1:1 coaching and group coaching, I leave with a deep sense of fulfillment, joy, and happiness. My clients and employees get great results and experience profound transformation from my coaching sessions. And in those moments of brightness, I knew in my core that coaching was my calling

Today I'm privileged to run a successful business, on my own terms. The truth is there is no overnight success formula. It takes time, energy, and willingness to fail forward and that's what it really takes to build a successful business that generates healthy profits and cash flow.

My vision for my business is to help entrepreneurs, professionals, and coaches to attract their dream clients and make money doing what they are passionate about. In both my own life and my clients', I have learned that one should not use money as your main motivation to build a business. The best reason for a business to exist in order to last is to serve others. According to Investopedia, about 90% of startups fail due to poor sales & marketing strategies and lack of business planning. The majority of them don't have an established customer base to serve. Be obsessed with the audience you want to serve so you can create endless ways to deliver value to your clients.

It's vital to build a business for the right reasons. If your heart is not there, people can feel it. You will not attract the right clients and retain them if you are missing joy, passion, or purpose in your business. Too many businesses fail from missing a deeper purpose for existence.

Next, an important key to "success" is to develop an alignment of your passion with your vision. Be honest with yourself, and take the time to analyse the true purpose for your business.

Rather than letting society dictate what success looks like, think and dream for yourself about what you want to achieve in your business. Decide how much you want to earn, what are your strengths, how many hours you want to work, and what kind of impact you will have on others. Tap into your own wisdom to visualise your dream business.

SUCCESS IS A JOURNEY...

So let me invite you to be BOLD. Be bold in being in your own skin. Be bold to show your true self to others. I hear you; it's not easy, and you fear judgement and criticism by others. I've been there too! But I promise you, there is only one of you on this earth.

Bold to do what's in your heart to serve others. Bold to take the risk so you can live a better life. Bold not to live under someone's shadow. Bold to own your uniqueness. Bold to speak up with grace, compassion and love. Bold to pursue all your dreams.

Love yourself deeply; when you love yourself more, you are able to love others more. Like attracts like, as goes the law of attraction. Love is the highest vibration that will send a frequency to others. Fill your cup overflowing with love. It's not selfish to love yourself. Love and approve yourself daily. Speak loving language to yourself. Nourish your body with food and hydrate your body. Exercise daily in ways that are fun, enjoyable and playful.

You're born with a unique set of gifts and talents. It's in your DNA. You may be utilising your gifts and talents now, but there's a strong possibility you may not be fully living your own uniqueness. Over the years, I did not have this opportunity because I was instead developing skills and abilities to build my career rather than my creativity and gifts. Take the time and embrace your own gifts and talents. To be successful in living your best life, you've got to be YOU.

Where do you start? Begin by exploring your own creativity. Allow your own mind to wander and daydream all your wildest dreams. Write them down in your journal. Feel the expansion of your heart, soul and mind as you give yourself the permission to explore your unique talents. Don't hold anything back as you listen to your higher self; let that inner voice guide you to do something you love. Take the time every day to be still and listen to your inner voice where it leads to new opportunities and see possibilities so you can be fully yourself. Don't judge your thoughts and ideas that come to you naturally. They are speaking to you to gently nudge you to pursue your own unique path of success. You have a brilliant mind that wants to unfold infinite possibilities to you so you can be successful. Let the success come from within you.

It's common to be uncomfortable with the topic of money. Money is energy and money is neutral. Here's an invitation to you to develop a healthy relationship with money. Speak well of money, as you would your friend. Nurture your money and manage the flow in and out with great wisdom. If you have a healthy friendship with money, money will flow to you with ease and grace. Become a money magnet by letting go of negative beliefs you may have been taught over the years. If you let go of outdated stories about money being hard to earn, rich people are evil, money doesn't grow on trees, now is the time to shift your relationship with money, because you so deserve to live a life of total abundance!

Time is an infinite resource. You get to decide how you want to use your time, so be present in the moment. Embrace every moment you've right now, don't think of the past or the future or you'll simply miss the present!

As I draw a close to my chapter, I'm inviting you to create your new future:

Visualise and journal all your deepest desires and dreams, there are no limits to it.

Let your mind wander and as your note down pen to paper, everything you desire in your heart, take a moment to pause and imagine yourself in that vision.

Experience how you feel, what you touch, the smells in the scene, notice the sound, and who are you surrounded by celebrating with you.

Everyone is so happy to be with you. You feel so safe and calm.

Deep down in your heart, you knew all the challenges you overcame were absolutely necessary, it is the surest way to reveal your own uniqueness and hidden gems, nothing can ever hold you back from your greatness,

Now it's your time to shine.

Believe all things are possible.

The truest form of success is like the butterfly effect.

ABOUT THE AUTHOR

JOCELYN CHONG

Jocelyn Chong is the Founder and CEO of Seed to Sequoia. After a 20 year successful career in the banking and finance world where she generated over $200 million in revenue, she quit her job to pursue her true passion as a life & business coach. Utilizing her MBA plus her background in high level sales, leadership and management, she has now worked with over 500 entrepreneurs and teaches them how to earn with ease, attract their dream clients, and create a life by design. Her mission is to help business leaders tap into their soul's calling and scale their business with feel good strategies & intuitive guidance. Jocelyn has been featured in Thrive Global, Digital Journal, FOX, Ask.com, The Times and Finance News World.

Website: www.jocelynchong.com.au
IG Handle: https://www.instagram.com/_jocelynchong_/
Facebook Handle: https://www.facebook.com/jocelyn.chong.9674
LinkedIn: www.linkedin.com/in/jocelynchong
Email me: jocelyn@jocelynchong.com.au

KELLY TAN

YOU HOLD THE POWER TO DEFINE YOUR SUCCESS

*T*his chapter is dedicated to my parents for being the light of my life and for encouraging me to share this story.

I have been carrying this secret around for years now.

A story that I have been too afraid to share.

And this has been a heavy weight on my shoulders.

But now is the time to tell my story because ...

I not only want women around the world to be inspired to take action and be in charge of their destiny,

But also to be empowered and know that they have the power within themselves to achieve and accomplish all that they desire.

And that woman is YOU!

I have fiercely fought to be the woman I am today:

Strong.

Resilient.

Tenacious.

Bold.

Independent.

Successful.

I'm here to share with you that you too can achieve what you want despite the nay-sayers and whatever situation you may be in. There's light at the end of the tunnel.

Wherever you are in your journey, you should know that you are supported, and that you have the power within you to claim your success.

Society has taught us that success is the amount you have in your bank account, fame, power, connections, status, the luxury brands you wear, the size of the house you live in, the staff you can afford to hire - the driver and nanny. It has been ingrained in me that this is what success looks like.

In magazines, you see titles of the top young entrepreneurs under 30 or lists of the 50 most successful people of the year, solely chosen because of the net worth these people have achieved. This has created an expectation that you need to achieve "success" within a short time—the shorter the better.

I grew up in a family of entrepreneurs. My father and brother had a business that provided a comfortable lifestyle. They each had their own sports cars, those fancy red machines, and an aeroplane. There was a photo on the wall for their remarkable accomplishments.

Every time I looked at that photo, I would see myself as a failure because I didn't have those fancy sports cars or that aeroplane.

A part of me felt like I disappointed my parents because I wasn't as successful as my brother. I struggled with feeling like I was lacking something within.

And so, this was how my entrepreneurship journey began. I wanted to achieve success, and did not give starting a business a second thought. There was no other way to the top.

Upon graduating from my tertiary education in Melbourne, Australia, the first thing I did was to start a beauty salon in Kuala Lumpur, Malaysia. I worked up to fourteen hours a day, six days a week. Even on rest days, I was running errands for the business.

If I wasn't running errands, I was reading on marketing and social media. I was brainstorming different strategies on how I could create a million-dollar business with a chain of beauty salons—one that would be a household name.

I didn't have the life of a normal twenty-four-year-old back then. There wasn't a time that I remember when I had any fun. My sole pursuit was work and to chase the dream of being successful. I missed out on social activities because I so deeply wanted that life.

My hard work paid off a few years later. I WAS SUCCESSFUL—as per the definition of society.

I was proud of my accomplishments. I was a very successful business owner of a prestigious multi-award-winning nail and waxing salon in Kuala Lumpur, Malaysia. Apart from that, I co-founded another waxing salon and was the founder of a beauty products supplier and hair removal education program.

I married my long-time boyfriend and we had a beautiful kid together. We traveled comfortably when we went on holidays, had good food and enjoyed a luxurious life.

Just in my twenties, I had it all.

But life was not all good. I was working long hours every day.

I was tired.

I was burnt-out.

I was lonely.

I felt so empty.

And I wondered, is this all that life has to offer?

I didn't have the time to spend with my family and parents and missed out on a lot of occasions or arrived very late. I was that girl in her twenties who didn't enjoy regular outings with friends because the conversations would be of different interests. I would rather be in the company of like-minded individuals talking about business, finance, or world news.

Along the way, I lost a part of myself. Because when I got to the top, I had no one to celebrate with. There wasn't a single person I could think of to call and shout "I did it! Let's celebrate!". Not even the person I was married to.

I got caught up in trying to chase the dream and wasn't happy. So, I made the decision to sell the salon. It took almost two years for an offer to come in. I remember it just like it was yesterday. I was in Melbourne on a holiday when I received a call from my broker that someone had put in an offer.

I said "yes", and the next thing I knew, I was on the plane back to sign the documents and finalize the sale. Putting my signature on that document was the hardest thing I ever had to do.

It was a business born out of passion and hard work. For those ten years, I had made women feel confident, well-groomed, and enjoyed the best experience. Some of them were not only customers but also became dear friends.

The saddest part was to say goodbye to the team I had. They were like family to me. I spent more time with them than I did with my family. They taught me more than I taught them. They taught me empathy, kindness, and what real hardship and resilience is. We celebrated moments and milestones.

One of them had been with me since I started the salon. She was my trusted and faithful employee, friend, and family. If you happen to read this book, you know who you are. Thank you for all that you have done for me. Once in a while, I say a little prayer for everyone.

After selling the salon, I stopped operating the rest of the businesses with no backup plan. I was extremely tired and felt the need to finally rest. The longest leave that I have ever taken was my maternity leave —one month to be exact.

Because of the extreme fatigue, I wanted to lean on my then-husband and spend the time at home with my son and my parents.

But still, the fear of losing my independence and being looked down on because I wasn't contributing to the family income stayed strong. I'm now glad I didn't make that choice, and this is why I'm sharing my story.

For a long time, my business defined me and created my identity. Everyone knew me as Kelly, the woman who had it all. I was afraid of stepping out of my shell.

A few months later, my marriage failed. For a long time, I couldn't tell anyone because having a failed marriage would have defined me as less successful.

Everything crumbled in an instant. I went on a journey of self-discovery. I did a lot of inner work to learn to love myself again and redefine what success is. Along the way, I discovered a spirituality that led me to be in alignment with myself.

The one thing that my parents taught me is to *never* give up. And for that, I thank them for constantly supporting me in this journey that led to what I've achieved today.

I started looking for jobs and was offered a position in a social media agency. Never in a million years would I have thought that I would work for someone else.

The thought of having to go through the process of a company deciding whether I am worthy enough to be part of their team irked me. The thought of having to build someone else's dream and not mine saddened me.

The income was nothing close to what I earned previously, and it took me a while to get comfortable with my newfound status. An employee with no freedom in time. I had to apply for leave if I wanted to take my son on a holiday or if I simply just wanted to spend the day with my parents. It was a huge adjustment.

But, that entrepreneur in me didn't die.

And so, I created an online side hustle. At that point, I was juggling between motherhood, working in an agency, and a side hustle. Again, I was almost on the verge of another burn-out. I knew, something had to go and that was my side hustle.

It never quite took off. It didn't turn out as expected because the online business world was so new to me and I didn't have the time to manage it.

Fortunately, I didn't give up on that dream of mine. Every day, I visualized having a business that would give me freedom and the ability to work from anywhere.

I gave it one last shot. I set an intention and worked so damn hard every day, understanding the processes and systems of how a social media agency worked, how to create a social media strategy, a plan, analyzing data, creating reports, and managing paid ads.

Luck didn't seem to be on my side. Despite being one of the most hardworking, responsible, and reliable employees, my role was deemed redundant because the agency had to cut back on its costs.

I was thrown into the wild of not knowing what to do next. It was a blow to my ego. At one point, I wanted to give up and just let go. Surrender to what the universe had planned for me. To just sit back, wait, and relax.

But, there was a fighting spirit in me that said, "Keep going". This was the turning point. I signed up and joined a few freelance platforms. Taking all my skills and experience from the agency I worked at, I started offering social media management and content creation services.

The first few months were tough because clients on these platforms were looking for someone who was experienced at the lowest rate possible.

Every day, I sent in my proposals. One day, a client hired me, and I had a sense of renewed hope and a boost of confidence. The ball started rolling and more clients came my way.

Soon, I had an impressive portfolio of clients. Eventually, I became one of the top-rated freelancers. I still work with some of the clients today.

With the hard work put in, my dream came true. I was able to work from anywhere at any time. I was traveling between Kuala Lumpur and Melbourne often.

My workplaces were frequently airport lounges and cafes. Some of the programs and services I offer today were even created on the plane. I had time to read books and watch movies. It was truly a dream that had come true.

I was once told my small little business wasn't an ambitious one, and that I wasn't getting anywhere in life. But really, this business survived and thrived, even through a pandemic.

This all happened because I believed in myself. I also happened to have a dear friend who constantly reminded me of how amazing I was. Jim Rohn once said that you are the average of the five people you spend the most time with. And so, these days I keep my circle of friends very small and selective only to those who are in alignment and have the same vibration as me.

Now, had I not decided to have independence and to just keep going, I would have lost myself and the capability to take care of my kid. It was that decision and path I took that led me to what I do today: to inspire and empower women to create their independence and write their own success story.

Don't let anyone, your job, or the materials you own define who you are. Prioritize having a backup plan even when you think you have the most perfect life. Anything can happen. It could be a failed marriage, a spouse getting laid off, or a family member who needs help.

You have the capability to provide and contribute. You have the independence to make decisions and have options in life, especially when you have children.

But let me remind you this: along the way, don't lose sight of what true success is. Most people define success as having the financial means and a luxurious lifestyle. I got it wrong. Society got it wrong. It's the other way around. Happiness is the core of success. Everything else in life is a bonus.

The most important tool to have is your mindset and how you define success. If you truly want to be successful, find your happiness first. It must come from within.

Fast forward a few years later, I now live in Melbourne, Australia, and am so grateful to be able to experience the culture and life here.

I founded Kelly Talks Social, a business with a vision and mission of helping women entrepreneurs create financial independence for themselves through my private and group coaching container, podcast, courses, and an online community.

I am now helping my community to take their business from zero to abundance so that they can enjoy freedom in business and life, be able to provide for themselves and family, have the option to enjoy better things in life without the stress and overwhelm, and to earn with ease. We prioritize happiness above it all.

I wake up every morning with joy to a balanced work-life lifestyle. My son and I have our morning gratitude ritual. The best part is when my son said to me one day, "Mumma, I'm grateful for you and I appreciate all that you do for me". Being able to impart wisdom and gratitude practice is success.

These days, my life looks a little something like this: client meetings, coaching calls, content creation, launching programs, collaborating with like-minded individuals, and meeting new friends. It's all fun without the burnout or unhappiness. I no longer feel the need to be happy only when I achieve X, Y or Z.

And what really lights me up is when I receive messages from my online community that I've inspired them in some way, shape, or form. That is success.

This feeling trumps the notification of a sale coming in. Don't get me wrong, I love that people support my work. It's the feeling of happiness knowing that my message is being seen and impacting lives around the world that truly lights me up.

Instead of working at the salon or an agency, I now get to spend time with the little one in the park after school and to see him run around with his friends with so much joy on his face. It is moments like this I live for. Occasionally, I get a beautiful flower from my little one that he plucked whilst playing with his friends.

I'm living life on my own terms, to the fullest and in the present. I get to do what I love every single day, helping one woman at a time. My aim in the next five years is to be on stages around the world to share my full story. This is only just a chapter of a story of a woman who rose from the darkness, reconstructed her path and redefined success.

With your permission, here's what I want to leave you with. When you are feeling low, I want you to remember this every day.

Don't ever let anyone or society define who you are...

If no one supports your dreams, you have the power to be your own cheerleader...

What you put out, you will attract ...

Be financially independent, have a backup plan because you'll never know what lies ahead. Don't ever settle ...

Having independence is fulfilling. And if you have kids, this shows them the power and strength within ...

Greatness is born out of belief ...

Happiness is the core of your success, everything else that comes along is a bonus ...

Once happiness is within you, all things will flow in with ease ...

That, my friend, is the success code. REDEFINED.

I invite you to close your eyes and say this out aloud...

I AM ENOUGH.

I AM AMAZING.

I AM A MASTERPIECE.

I BELIEVE IN MYSELF.

I AM POWERFUL

I AM UNSTOPPABLE.

I AM SUCCESSFUL.

CLAIM IT.

And as I finish writing this chapter, the weight has lifted off my shoulders. I have never been able to share this story for the fear of people judging or being seen as a failure. I now see things differently. There is power in my story because I know that others will find solace and draw inspiration from it.

Keep shining bright.

ABOUT THE AUTHOR

KELLY TAN

Kelly Tan is the founder of Kelly Talks Social and has over ten years of social media experience as a Social Media and Content Coach who helps coaches and service-based entrepreneurs navigate through challenges and overwhelm using social media. Previously, she built an award-winning beauty salon over ten years through the power of social media. She is a certified nail technician, waxing therapist, barista, and foodie. Kelly was driven by the need to help business owners attract more clients and earn with ease. Her mission is to inspire and empower women entrepreneurs to rise up and enjoy independence and freedom in both business and life. Kelly has helped many business owners with proven strategies and tools to turn their business from zero to abundance using 1:1 coaching, masterclasses, courses and digital products. Kelly lives in Melbourne, Australia with her son, Xander.

Website: https://kellytalkssocial.com/
Instagram: https://www.instagram.com/kellytalkssocial/
Facebook: https://www.facebook.com/kellytalkssocial
Facebook Group: www.facebook.com/
groups/socialmediaonlinetraining/
LinkedIn: www.linkedin.com/in/kellytaneli/
TikTok: https://www.tiktok.com/@kellytalkssocial?
Pinterest: https://www.pinterest.com.au/kellytalkssocial/

Clubhouse: kellytalksocial
Podcast: https://podcasts.apple.com/us/podcast/kelly-talks-social/id1523700908
Email: kelly@kellytalkssocial.com

13

KRISTI HRIVNAK

SUCCESS IS BEING

I grew up with an attachment to success. I lived and breathed under the illusion that success had something I did not. My belief systems were tangled in the ideal that success was a concept, something outside of me. So, I made it my inner life mission to obtain status, money and accolades in order to receive its power. However, each time I achieved some form of success, no sooner did I achieve it that I was already looking for the next level of it. Each level I reached soon became the new baseline for the next achievement.

One day, I asked myself, where was the power in this way of living? If success had power and I had achieved so many things, shouldn't I then feel powerful? At this point, shouldn't I be a walking talking embodiment of the power of success? Instead, I felt empty inside. I was experiencing a complete lack of power. Logically, I knew I was successful. I could see on paper all I had achieved in life and recognize I had already done more than many people will in a lifetime. However, emotionally, I felt completely void of the sensation of success.

My entire existence was entangled in a false concept of success. Subconsciously, I believed success was something outside of me to be obtained. The chase for success was something I relied on to fuel a part of me that was void of love and acceptance. Even in the many moments of achieving success, that void was never filled. A lack of love cannot be filled by anything other than love. I was headed down a rabbit hole that had no end. The more I attempted to fill myself up from the outside in, the more obvious my inner emptiness became.

The attachment to an ideal is not unique to me. The majority of society walks around with their own tangled, twisted relationship with success. Of course we each define this relationship through our own terms, but at its core it is still linked to something outside of the self. This includes a person's identity. The identity that we each occupy in this life exists outside of the Self. As a result, the success we obtain to fuel our identity is different than a measure of true success. That is where most of us have gotten confused about what success truly is.

Success to satisfy the identity is an outward motion of success. Success to satisfy the true Self is an inward motion of success. This shift in understanding is what completely altered my perception of success, my relationship to the concept of success and my life itself.

As I began to look at success in terms of an inward journey, I established a deep sense of wholeness and an appreciation for who I am. I met myself on a level that I had not previously known. I encountered parts of myself I had hidden from the world. I was reacquainted with parts of myself that had long been forgotten. I discovered parts of myself I had never known were there. This inward journey into the depths of my soul gave me a sense of power I had never experienced through any external form of success.

After years of walking this inward path, committed to letting go of any and all attachment to the external world I opened up to a reality I never could have conceived in my own mind. All of the inner work I had accomplished provided a deep sense of success and personal power I had never known. I truly discovered who I really am: a clear channel for Divine wisdom and guidance.

With that, I will surrender the remainder of this chapter to my higher self and the collective of energy beings that I work with, and allow their wisdom, truth and compassion to offer an insight into success that we may all benefit from for the highest good.

As you read these words, you can become aware of your breath. You can feel the air flowing in and out of the body. You can notice that your body doesn't need to be told how to breathe or when to breathe. Your breathing is easy and effortless. There is a graceful flow as the air moves into every cell and makes its way back out again. This is the epitome of success.

We are here to remind you that you need not reach far for success. True success is in you. You are success. The fact that you are living and breathing in this very moment means you are contributing to the success of life and all of humanity. Of course there are many ways you would like to further contribute to the world but that doesn't mean you are void of success until you do those things. Here and now, you are successful.

Your human mind finds this hard to believe. In fact, it desires not to believe this at all. The mind is trained to look for what is not rather than for what is. We know that you know how much your mind likes to complicate the simplest things in life. Success is just the kind of thing the mind takes great pleasure in complicating. The mind loves to have a problem to solve; so, it first must create a problem like a lack of success so it can proceed to solve it.

If you could see what we see, you would not question if there is anything else you need to be, do or have in order to be considered successful. You are it. Success is not something that is outside of you. Success is in you and all around you. Now, you may have difficulty *feeling* success but that does not mean it is not there. Just as when you are feeling sad, you may have difficulty accessing love. Your difficulty in accessing love does not mean that there is an absence of love.

Perhaps you are wondering how you can access the success that you already are. And we are here to tell you that you are doing it right this second. As you breathe and as you read, you may feel the quiet vibration of success within you. Deep inside each and every cell there is a success for simply being alive.

We would like you to take a moment and consider how many synchronicities and moments had to happen in the world for you to be conceived. Just think, for a moment of everything that needed to align just so you could be conceived and later born into this world. The path and the buildup to the moment of your birth was like a journey to the highest mountain peak. There, you came into this world at the very top of the mountain. That is where you started this life. You came into this world a miraculous masterpiece simply being in your existence.

As time went on and you made your way through different life experiences, your mind began to complicate things. Your emotional guiding system and your thought patterns began to reject the simplicity of the concept of success. You created a story that success is something else. Success became something outside of you, something you lack that you need to obtain. This illusion caught your attention and you have been working to realize an illusory concept ever since.

We are here to help you dispel this illusion within your being. You are a soul. You are the expansive, infinite energy of love and light. You are also, temporarily, a human. You are a clearly defined body with limitations, boundaries and an identity. The way your soul knows success is different than the way your human defines success. We desire for you to come to an understanding of success that integrates these two seemingly contradictory concepts. In doing so, you will find a way to live life that embodies success in every moment, while still allowing you to expand in the physical world as you so desire.

According to your soul, which is where we are speaking to you from, there is no moment when you are not successful. The soul exists beyond space and time. So, if there is no concept of time in the realm of the soul, there can't possibly be any moment when you are not the epitome of success. If there is no concept of space in the realm of the soul, you can't possibly need to be anywhere other than here and now for you to experience success.

According to your human form, there are things you desire that you do not already have, and in this linear way of thinking that makes you not yet successful. Your human exists within a space-time reality. So, if time is a real concept there are moments when you are successful and moments when you are not successful. Your human also exists in space and oftentimes must move through space by way of experience to arrive at the next moment of success.

From being and existing in these two very different realities, you can see why a very simple concept like success has gotten tangled into something it is not. As we dissect the word here with you, we trust you will also experience a disentangling of energy within you around the idea of success. We would love for you to regain a sense of clarity in your being with which you can lead yourself into the next chapter of your life.

To disentangle the energy around success, you must understand this idea of mutual inclusivity. Two seemingly contradictory parts can co-exist at the same time. Many of you logically know this but do not necessarily live this in your being. To embody this idea means to experience life in embracing the moment-to-moment success that is already in you, while at the same time moving toward more success in the physical world.

Which brings us to presence. Presence is how you access the success that you are in this moment. Presence and just simply *being* are where you can truly connect with who you really are: a soul having a human experience. Presence is what you are experiencing as you read these words and spend this time here with us. We are so grateful you are here. We love seeing you immersed in the presence of your life. We love when you deepen beyond the bodymind and find that place of oneness in whatever you are doing. This is success. You already know how to be in this energy. More and more you may give yourself permission to just be.

As you embrace the present and remember the success that you already are, you will begin to notice an integration of human and soul. Spending more time in the present, attuning to the success already in you, begins to open the doors for the physical world success your human self desires.

You might wonder how this is possible. You may ask how physical measures of success can possibly come to you without relying solely on the human mind and what it knows to be true; that success requires planning, hard work and persistence. We are here to show you that embracing this possibility is only a matter of perspective. When you let go of the human mind, even for a moment, you open up to pure possibility and unlimited potentiality. The space between every thought you have within the mind, opens up into a vast, infinite space where anything can be birthed.

Inspiration, creativity, motivation, excitement, breakthroughs, epiphanies are all birthed from the present. Since we know this is true, we also know that there is an unlimited amount of power at your disposal in the present moment. Which means every time you are stuck in the mental and emotional limitations of the human mind, you are not in a place of accessing this power.

So, the picture is starting to become clearer. You have two parts, the soul and the human. Each of these parts understands success differently. The way to access both definitions of success simultaneously is through presence. The way to experience presence is to simply be immersed in the moment you are in without analyzing, planning or controlling it.

The more you become present, the more you have access to unlimited potentials that exist for you. The more you gain access to these unlimited potentials, the more Divine resources you are able to receive. The more Divine resources you are able to receive, the more expanded you become as a human being. The more expanded you become, the more powerful you become.

Here we are back at this word 'power', which is so beautifully linked with success. When you access your own internal power through ongoing commitment to the present moment you begin to interact differently with the world. The relationship your human self has with the world is of a limited, physical understanding. The human self understands linear progression that, with constant effort through time and space, a result is inevitable.

The relationship your soul has with the world is of an expanded, limitless understanding. From the eyes of the soul, there are an infinite number of ways to arrive at a specific result, and they are all accessible in the present. To own your power is to understand your own personal balance and alignment for these two philosophies.

Your alignment will be unique to you. Some of you may feel more powerful with a more linear approach to your life lead by the human self. Others may feel more powerful with a more circular approach lead by the soul. The important thing to understand is your power comes from honoring both pieces of you. You will never be just one or the other. You will always be both. It is your duty to live life from a place that honors the human and the soul. Living from this aligned place is where physical world success will find you.

We feel we have said everything we need to say but there is still a lingering feeling of something being undone. There are some people reading whose human self desires to understand more deeply. The human mind in all its beauty is looking for a way to apply the teachings to your life. The mind is efforting in order to grasp at something you are not.

We don't wish for you to worry yourself about this concept of success or anything you have read that you don't currently understand. All that does is keep you out of the present, which as we now know is where your success is. We desire for you not to take a concept like success and make it bigger than who you are.

You are the one. This version of you reading this book, right here, right now, is everything. This is all you need to be for success to find you in the physical reality. The more your human self embraces this truth and the more you remember who you already are; a walking, talking miracle moving your way through life, the faster the physical success you desire will find you.

So, rest easy. Breathe. Bring your awareness to your inhales and your exhales. Observe the contraction and expansion of your diaphragm and chest as you breathe. Feel how relaxing it is just to be here now perfectly connected and aligned with your human and your soul. We are so happy you chose to share this moment with us. We know you got exactly what you needed from these words and will continue to get everything you need from the other chapters in the book.

We love you.

ABOUT THE AUTHOR

KRISTI HRIVNAK

Following the sale of her first business, CrossFit Vortex, Kristi Hrivnak uncovered a unique inner gift in remote energy healing. By combining her sensitivity as an intuitive empath along with her previous knowledge of the mind-body connection, Kristi helps people clear emotional trauma and accelerate inner growth.

Kristi graduated with a BSc in Kinesiology, an MBA, finished in the top 2% in her athletic endeavors, and has been published several times in Mindbodygreen. However, her more recent discoveries in energy work and trusting her soul's calling are by far her biggest accomplishment to date.

Kristi continues to fine-tune her gift while working for the greater good of the planet. She offers powerful healing journeys and shares daily channeled messages through her Miracle Messenger Instagram platform. She looks to the future with an openness, ready to serve and make an impact in whatever way her soul calls.

Website: www.kristihrivnak.com
Instagram: https://www.instagram.com/kristi.hrivnak
https://www.instagram.com/miracle.messenger
Facebook: www.facebook.com/kristi.hrivnak/

14

LINDSAY RAE D'OTTAVIO

THE BOTTOM LINE IS YOU ARE EXACTLY AS YOU ARE MEANT TO BE

*M*y grandparents opened the first photography studio in Miami in 1951. "Fine Arts Photography" was run by my uncle Lewis up until COVID-19 in 2020 forced closure.

My early childhood began in a family which I believed to be relatively wealthy. We lived on a cul-de-sac in a gated community; Dan Marino from the Miami Dolphins lived a few streets down.

I'm sharing this with you through the eyes a very young girl. I recall walking into my house and seeing the pink marble floors, green granite countertops, the huge pool out back. I also remember losing it all. The same girl who experienced this simultaneously watched it all slip away.

Over the course of only a few years, my family had gone from life in the big house to a modest townhome; from the modest townhome to a cramped two-bedroom apartment inhabited by my five person family. By this point, my younger brother and sister shared a small bedroom while the living room sofa became my bedroom each night. The next time I would have a real bed to sleep in each night wasn't until age nineteen when I moved myself to Manhattan.

I recall the feelings of preparing to graduate high school and not being able to afford a cap and gown. My friends each contributed $10 to help pay for the symbolic garments of this rite of passage so many usually take for granted. Honestly, one I would have taken for granted as the young girl who had not known this life which awaited her. This was a distinct low point in my life. But it was yet to be my lowest.

Looking back at myself as a young woman, I now recognize that my self-worth was almost entirely defined by what I believed other people thought of me. As a result, the unending quest to seek their validation and approval superseded my own needs, feelings, wants and led to patterns of self-neglect in the process. I received a scholarship to a NYC-based college my senior year after winning Best in Show Monologue at our district thespian competition. What was one of my proudest, most significant moments of accomplishment to date ultimately took a back seat to a boy—one who had no interest in committing to me or the relationship. Even so, I elected to turn down the scholarship and this opportunity for a brighter future to instead stay in Florida and be by his side as long as he'd have me.

Then, there was the accident: the one that changed it all for me, my perspective on life, on me within it. I relive that drive vividly: what I was wearing, the stamp on my hand from the club, the fear that stamp would give responding officers the notion I had been drinking despite being completely sober. I will never forget the feeling of powerlessness as a Florida squall struck and I lost control of my vehicle. Picture this: I'm nineteen, glittery mini-dress, wrapped around a tree during a torrential downpour, in an unregistered and unmarked car. It would take me nineteen years to overcome the trauma around the accident and a severe fear of driving before I would get behind the wheel again at thirty-two.

Sitting in the seat of my mangled vehicle, stunned, I recognized how narrowly I had just escaped an early exit from life before getting the chance to truly live it. The clarity of this realization gave me a new desire seize life, one I had all but decided was in the cards for others but never for me. The following day, I set the wheels to a different life in motion. I called the college and told them my story, requesting another chance to attend their program with the scholarship I had turned down. They awarded part of it back and the rest was up to me. Within two weeks, I earned $1,800 in the phone room I had been working at with my mother, and used the money for my plane ticket to New York City and the first investment in myself, my worth, and my happiness. I didn't know how I was going to make it work, but I got my first credit card, rented a place sight unseen, packed my bags and embarked on a new future with the conviction I would find a way.

I was chasing my dreams and took my first big step towards betting on me, but I was still nineteen years old in a brand-new city with no money, no self-worth, and the damages of a youth I had not yet begun to understand the depths of. The best was still yet to come, but not without some of the greatest hurdles and obstacles I would face to date.

Fast forward a year to being twenty years old in Manhattan, losing the first dream job I'd landed, maxing out all of the credit cards I had taken out, and feeling the crushing weight of desperation and hopelessness begin to engulf me once more. This was the setting of my next brush with death, but this time by my own design. I felt completely alone, worthless, doomed to a life of failures and unmet expectations. As I inched step by step to the edge of the bridge over the river drowning in a sea of toxic self-talk, my phone rang. My friend Adam was on the other end of the line. He literally talked me off the ledge, bought me a plane ticket back to Florida, and helped me ground me back into a reality where this was not going to be the end, not by a long shot. Instead, I got on that plane and spent the next six months recuperating and planning how to tackle the next phase of life, armed with the experiences and lessons learned.

It was during this time that I began to start filling my toolbox with some real, healthy, sustainable tools for life. I have since learned how to apply these in both personal as well as professional endeavors and utilize them to support living my best self in all aspects of life.

One such tool which I value highly today was meditation. If you struggle with the word "meditation" as I have, you can feel free to call it "brainstorm time". Call it anything really, as long as it's dedicated time which allows you to become open to the benefits. It can be frou-frou, it can be a religious experience. Or not. It is whatever you want it to be for you and your own needs.

My morning routine these days includes an hour to drive through the farm towns and take the winding back roads of upstate New York, music turned up, cruise control without a destination in mind, immersed in my own "brainstorm time". This is my brand of meditation as it incorporates mindfulness while centering and bringing clarity where it's needed for the noise upstairs. My mind is focused on the road, on driving defensively and safely as my vehicle traverses the turns, dips, hills and, well, occasional pot holes! This allows me to explore and process all of the business between my ears while not getting swept away by it and escalating to a place of anxiety, fear and self-defeating thinking. By having to remain physically present and focused on the act of driving and the environment around me, I am free to navigate my mind in a safe and productive manner which will support my goals for the day at home and at work.

Learning to sit with my thoughts and face them without fear has been one of the greatest challenges of my life, but it is hands-down the biggest catalyst to my success. I've learned the importance of asking myself questions: "Why are you feeling this? What do you want from this?"

The peak shift required to grow my business into a profitable six-figures has been the ability to sit with my emotions rather than run from them. The process of building your own business is a rewarding but taxing, emotional experience. This is inevitable and ultimately cannot be outrun or avoided. Pay special attention to feelings of jealousy, jealousy towards other entrepreneurs, towards their successes. Recognize that this feeling likely stems from personal doubts, fears, insecurities, and instead try to identify and learn from their success to inform your own journey.

Questioning my worth, my value, my beauty, my abilities has been a lifelong struggle which has been crucial for me to work on overcoming as I journey towards living my best self and continuing to grow a profitable and thriving brand. I came from an emotionally and physically abusive household. From my earliest memories, I recall my father constantly telling me I wasn't good enough. He would give me a list of the things that I would need to do in order to fulfill his version of someone who is worthy of respect. I was only beautiful if I could lose weight. I was only smart if I read the books that he wanted. I was only welcome in his new home with his new family if I was willing, like him, to become a born-again Christian. The list was endless.

Today, I know for a fact I am not alone. I have photographed close to 700 women, most of whom come to me to strip down both emotionally and physically, seeking to confront their own insecurities and negative tapes playing in their heads. Women on the same quest to find love for themselves as they are, in their own bodies.

I now recognize the important truth of how similar we are, and how my insecurities, negative self-talk, questionable self-worth is hardly unique to me. This has freed me from the self-imposed mind prison I believed I was alone in for so long. In reality, it is part of the human experience to grow up receiving messages from people and a society which tells us we are only "good enough if".

I've never had a size two client come in happy with themselves. She wishes she had curves like me, while I wish I was slender like her. We have been forced to believe that the only way that we can be good enough is if we can look like a Photoshopped version of a person. We have been ushered into adulthood by generations who believed tearing someone down as the peak means of building strength and resilience.

When my daughter, Gaia, was born in 2013, I had a very normal postpartum body after an emergency C-section. But I remember countless mornings logging onto Facebook and getting lost in a torrent of profile pictures of new mothers who seemingly bounced right back and lost the baby weight right after childbirth. I would open up my Facebook Messenger daily to a barrage of messages from different 'MLM huns' telling me all the ways they could help me lose weight and get back my pre-baby body so I'd find myself beautiful and worthy again.

I am here to tell you what they never taught us in school: Our worth is contingent on no one but ourselves. We enter this world worthy of respect and love, and we leave this world worthy of respect and love. It took me nineteen years and four major confrontations with myself before I finally believed my own peace and worth were real, and that I was entitled to them without apology. These four conflicts have steered the course of my entire life.

Do not blame yourself for being insecure in your skin. We all are. We come from the generation that created Photoshop, special effects, new makeup and an entire industry that was built upon destroying your confidence so they can sell you things to build it back up. I'm telling you today you are not alone facing the enemy you believe you see in the mirror.

You do not have to love yourself today, but today you can begin taking the first step towards what you will do to like yourself just a little bit more tomorrow.

Is that cleaning up your social media by deleting people who make you feel bad about yourself? Is it cleaning out your closet and getting rid of the jeans you know will never fit you again (the ones which belong to the body of a girl who has not yet become a woman)? It took many years before I was able to stand naked in front of the mirror and be okay with what I saw.

Next, "clean house" to support your emotional health and well-being. For me, I have not talked to my dad in almost two years, and it's the best decision that I've ever made. I've also recently gone through my phone and deleted anybody and everybody who was not good for me, including the people who brought me down, the people who wanted to hold me back, and the people whose envy was too loud for their love to overcome. I look at the affirmation I have adorning a post-it note on my mirror each morning: "The dead ends have to go so you can grow". Just like hair, making cuts and changes after so many years of the same thing can be hard to do. We get attached to what we have known for so long, much like family members or childhood friends which have long since been toxic for us. People say that blood is thicker than water, but I don't buy it. If you are not finding the support and love you deserve from your family of origin, find it in your family of choice. Space in my life is earned not through blood, but through actions.

Another key to building a pathway to success lies in setting and reinforcing my own while simultaneously respecting others' healthy boundaries.

Memorize this: "Do you have the emotional capacity right now to talk? I could use a friend." Healthy boundaries are a two-way street. Do not expect others to respect and adhere to your boundaries if you are not working to do the same in return.

Another incredibly powerful tool is visualization. I love using symbolism as part of my vision-work. Picture each obstacle to your success as a wall. What are you willing to do to get beyond the wall and break through to your goals and dreams on the other side? Will you dig a hole under this metaphorical wall? Will you climb over it? Will you walk twenty miles to find a way around it? If what is on the other side means enough to you, what won't you do to reach it?

I also look at my anxiety with symbolism. I imagine the little green booger from the Mucinex commercial as the embodiment of each of my fears. It's hard to get crippled or defeated by fear when a green blob with TJ Miller's voice pops up in your head!

Perhaps the greatest obstacle I have faced in adulthood and as an entrepreneur is financial insecurity. I hold a lot of fear around money. As mentioned earlier, I began early childhood in a family with means which was ultimately lost, in large part due to my father's fiscally irresponsible choices. My father's spending was largely to find extrinsic means of validation and worth as a superficial substitute for meaningfully intrinsic self-worth. With the loss of his money, my father left us in search of a "do-over" with a new life, new wife and new family. For the next twenty years of my life, my dad jumped from job to job in his quest to avoid paying my mother child support. We became riddled with so much debt that the elementary school crossing guard began collecting canned goods for us, and I would eat Hormel chili almost every night of the week for dinner on top of potatoes that had been growing spud eyes.

My mom went on to tell me the biggest mistake in her twenty-seven years of marriage wasn't that she trusted my father with money, which of course she counted highly among them, but most of all that she didn't "squirrel away" anything for herself. People say in a marriage you should share everything as a tenet of trust, yet paying yourself is not a devaluation of trust. When fear can dictate your money, fear has officially won. Assert your value to your partner and advocate to put away something each month, even if just a little bit.

My friend, Laura, laughs because of the squirrel analogy. She says, "Why be a squirrel when you can be a crow? Crows get what they need and fly away." Be a crow! Collect your shiny objects (and accomplishments), then fly away and build a nest in a place where you are accepted, loved and supported.

I grew my business over six years and went from making $30,000 yearly to $675,000 during a global pandemic. The key ingredient to my success has been acknowledging my worth and choosing to invest in myself. When you truly believe in your worth, a risk becomes an investment in your continued future success.

As I end this chapter and leave you to the other fantastic women who will take you on a spiritual journey, I hope you will challenge yourself to make that personal investment you have been hesitant to seize. Remember, when you learn to face your fears and boldly face the obstacles between you and what you want, you will see yourself in a new beautiful light of your own creation and realize there's absolutely nothing that can stop you.

You are worthy of success exactly as you are.

ABOUT THE AUTHOR
LINDSAY RAE D'OTTAVIO

Lindsay Rae is an internationally published and a multi-award winning photographer and inspirational speaker, including first place for Professional Boudoir at RangeFinder's Celebrate the Body competition and the 2021 Speaker Slam on Self-Acceptance, North America's largest speaking competition.

Lindsay owns and operates Self Love Experience out of Troy, New York. Her work has been published in Times Union, Shutterbug Magazine, Period Magazine, Voltron Magazine, and Ellements Magazine. Lindsay is also an active contributor to Women's Business Daily and Brainz Magazine.

From a difficult upbringing in a family on welfare to building a multiple six-figure business selling her art in New York, Lindsay's focus is on self-love, self-confrontation, overcoming body insecurity, and seeing yourself as more than scars of your past.

Lindsay believes confidence in the skin you are in trickles into every aspect and relationship in your life, and she gives women permission to feel beautiful exactly as they are.

Instagram: https://www.instagram.com/thebodyimageactivist/
Facebook: https://www.facebook.com/LindsayRaePhoto
Facebook Group: https://www.facebook.com/groups/lrpboudoirgroup
Email: Lindsay@bodyimageactivist.com

15

LIZ COALTS

PRETTY DAMN SUCCESSFUL RIGHT NOW

*I*t was quite a shock to me when I realized that it has been twenty years since I graduated high school. I am frequently in disbelief that the 1990's were not ten years ago. Movies and albums I love were released 25 years ago. This time has gone by fast. I was always told it would, but nothing really prepared me for time whooshing by. While I am shocked it has been twenty years since I officially embarked onto adulthood, I am also not surprised by how fast the years have gone by, because I packed those years with the pursuit of success. Since I walked across the stage in a cap in gown and received my high school diploma, I have earned an undergraduate degree, got married, started a career, bought a house, earned an MBA while working full time, had a child, received promotions, had another child, sold my house, moved to a new state, bought a new house, left my career, and started a business. A series of achievements that I have always associated with being successful.

The problem is, somewhere along the way, I correlated achieving success with happiness. Achieving these milestones and achieving this success would make me happy. As I have journeyed through these last twenty years, I was constantly seeking the next success.

Once I graduate from college and get a good job, I will be happy. I will be happy because I will be successful.

Once I become a real adult and get married, have a house and kids I will be successful (and therefore happy).

Once I get the promotion, I will earn more money and be successful (and happy).

> Success = college, career, marriage, children
> College + career+ marriage + children = Happiness
> Success = Happiness

As I went along this path, I would expect that when I achieved one of these 'successes', I would automatically transform into feeling like a success and being happy. But this was not always true. I achieved the outcomes, but I would always want more. I would find myself disappointed that achieving this milestone would not produce happiness or feeling successful.

So now, taking a critical look back over the last two decades, I am *not* shocked by the severe battles I have had with depression and anxiety. I had linked success with happiness, and then when I did not automatically "achieve" happiness, I thought that it meant I had not found the right thing to succeed at yet. This would just lead to a constant spiral of hoping that my next achievement will make me happy followed by disappointment time and time again.

Success is a noun, succeed is a verb, but I always expected success to equal happiness. In my mind, successful people were happy. Successful people went to college, had a high-paying job, a house, are married, have children. But what I found was as I achieved those successes that I was not automatically happier. So many of those accomplishments, while happy and hard earned, bring on stressors of their own. It is probably worth noting that Merriam-Webster did not define happiness as achieving success.

I also had the notion that these "successes" needed to be achieved in a straight line, which just fueled my anxiety when my carefully laid plans to reach those milestones fell off the path.

So, in 2010, when I found myself with a college degree, MBA, secure job, marriage, house, and a baby, the depression completely threw me off-kilter. The happiness that was supposed to come with the achievement of these things was not there. Depression was not part of the equation.

Instead of using the knowledge, skills, and abilities I had gained over approximately twenty-eight years of life, education, and jobs, I believed that there must be something else that I needed to achieve and succeed at to bring happiness. Was it the next level of a salary? Was it a promotion? Was it being a director? Should I get another degree? Successful people had these things and successful people are happy so I must just be missing something that I needed to achieve. I hid my depression and continued to strive for more.

I do not recall the exact moment, though most likely sometime after my hospitalization in a psych ward, that I had the realization that I needed to learn to love my life the way I have it. This was not an overnight occurrence. It is not something I am perfect at right now. But I started choosing to work at happiness and to stop relying on achievements to bring that happiness.

One key lesson I have learned along the way is that you must define what success means to YOU to be happy when you achieve that success. In addition, how you achieve YOUR success must also be in the way that is best for YOU. If you are pursuing goals because they are someone else's definition of success, or it is the tried-and-true path to achieve that goal, you will most likely not be happy once you achieve the success of meeting that goal. You will end up feeling resentful, tired, tricked, foolish, and ultimately unsuccessful.

As I am writing this, it is Sunday morning. It is pouring rain and I am drinking coffee sitting on my back porch. In this moment, I am in a state of contentment. This is a pleasurable and satisfying experience. It meets Merriam-Webster's definition of happiness. Yet, writing on the porch is not what I would have considered a typical measure of success, but it is making me happy in this moment.

Success means to turn out well. In my opinion, this Sunday morning did turn out well.

It is important to hold success to a literal measurement: Has the goal been achieved or not? But the distinction is to not tie your happiness or self-worth to the achievement of that success. Happiness is not, should not, be limited to a yes or no response. It is a range. It is on a spectrum. I am incredibly happy on this rainy Sunday morning. I am also happy when my family comes to visit me in my new home state. I was happy when my daughter played catcher for the first time in softball because Mommy was a catcher. It makes me happy seeing my younger daughter concentrate intensely on the complicated martial arts patterns she has memorized. I am happy when I see my husband driving his Jeep with the doors off in the warm North Carolina air, because I know it has been a dream of his for years. Yes, I was happy to receive my MBA or a promotion, but I have also been happy in all other moments in my life.

Meeting a goal you have set for yourself is the very definition of success. Achieving a goal is not the definition of happiness. Keep that in mind.

Happiness can equal success and success can lead to happiness, but the key is you must define what both happiness and success mean to you. You need to know what you are striving for, and you need to know (and believe in) the why behind striving towards it.

Why do I want to pursue this goal? Why it is important to me? Why am I trying to achieve this goal? Why am I trying to achieve this goal in this way? If you find yourself with subpar answers when you ask yourself why, maybe it means that the goal you are trying to achieve is someone else's goal. Achieving someone else's goal might lead to the success of achieving that goal, but it will not guarantee you happiness.

On a page, it may sound simple but it is anything but. It has taken me years to reach this point, and I am constantly checking with myself about what goals I am working towards and why. Looking at my goals and what I am working towards, I ask myself, "Why am I working towards this? What am I hoping to achieve?" For example, I have my own consulting and coaching business, and I am working towards the goal of having complete control over my schedule. Here is what my why's look like:

I want to have complete control over my schedule.

Why?

Because I do not want to have to ask for time off and hope it gets approved.

Why?

Because I want a flexibility to balance my kids' busy schedules, travel to see my family, make self-care a priority, and have an income to support my life.

I am working towards this goal of complete control over my schedule because I believe it will lead me to more flexibility. I think that having this flexibility will bring more peace to my life because I will not feel constrained to doing enjoyable happy things outside of Monday-Friday 9-5. The important part I need to keep remembering is that being successful in reaching this goal will not automatically equate to happiness. I think that I will have less stress and more space in my life to do the things I enjoy, which, will allow more space for happiness and make it easier to recognize each day. You cannot wait for happiness; you must see it where you are.

Before I started my own business, I had a well-paying, secure, government job. I had been there for fifteen years and had to work eighteen more years to retire with a full pension. Through my time there, I had discovered I had a passion for sharing my story and helping others, a passion for writing, and generally a passion for lots of things that I was not doing each day in this government job. I knew that I could wait until I was fifty-five to pursue the things I was passionate about. I had gone so far down this safe path, and knew that staying in this job for eighteen more years was the safe, responsible thing to do. But something always bothered me; it seemed like so many people at my job were living just to retire. They counted down the years, days, and hours until that magical retirement day. And yes, that magical, well-deserved day came for so many of them. But there were also many reminders that life is too short. People who would never get to retire, or people who retired only to pass away a few years later. Once I started paying attention to this, I could not unsee it and I could not shake how unhappy I was. Despite all my success and achievements that brought me to that place, I was unhappy.

When my family and I made a huge life change of moving from New York to North Carolina, I also took that opportunity to step away from my job. I had the opportunity to continue working remotely for at least a year, if not longer, due to COVID. But I chose not to. I chose to start pursuing my own business. It was scary. People probably thought it was a stupid decision. But I have not regretted my decision yet.

Am I in total control of my schedule right now? No. I am consulting for clients in hourly and retainer packages, and they require me to generally be available during 'normal' business hours.

But am I on my way to more flexibility? Yes.

And does this mean that my happiness needs to wait until I achieve this full control over my schedule? No.

Happiness is a practice. A practice of being in a state of well-being or contentment. Happiness is a choice, not an achievement. This lesson has been extremely challenging for me. Sometimes I stumble and think achieving success will make me happy. Sometimes I straight up fail at being happy with my life the way I have it. So, as I sit here now editing this chapter, after working nine hours for clients, my girls are coloring in my office, listening to Christmas music in June. They are singing and content, just being in the same room as me. Instead of being annoyed and stressed at not being left alone 'in peace to write', I am choosing to smile and be happy in this moment. I feel pretty damn successful right now.

ABOUT THE AUTHOR

LIZ COALTS

Liz Coalts is the owner of the Anxious Adult, LLC. She is a consultant and coach who helps smart but overwhelmed adults manage the anxieties of business and life using systems, processes, and metrics. Liz believes that anxiety should not hold a person back from achieving their big goals and dreams. She openly shares her stories of struggles with depression, anxiety, and imposter syndrome to show others how they can be successful despite setbacks. Liz has been featured in the *This Is My Brave* NYC show and on the *Darkside of the Full Moon* podcast. She holds an MBA and has over fifteen years of experience as an analyst, project manager, and leader. Liz is originally from Albany, New York and currently lives with her husband and two daughters in Raleigh, North Carolina.

Website: www.theanxiousadult.com
Instagram: www.instagram.com/ecoalts
Facebook: https://www.facebook.com/theAnxiousAdult
Facebook Group: www.facebook.com/groups/theanxiousadult/
LinkedIn: https://www.linkedin.com/in/liz-coalts/
Email: Liz@theanxiousadult.com

16

MARIKO BRENNER

SUCCESS IS MAGNETIC: YOU CAN'T HUSTLE
YOUR WAY INTO ALIGNMENT

*It is my responsibility to share my great work with the world.
~Gabrielle Bernstein*

My story is about remembering. Remembering my voice, that I am powerful beyond measure. It is about recognizing I am already whole and complete. Remembering being enough, worthy, and deserving of love and juiciness.

I've always been different, my own person. Even as a child, no one could make me do anything I did not want to do. My soul wants the space and freedom to sit by the river and gaze off into the distance, space for life to be a poetic song filled with travel to many places and experiences. My body aches for connection, to express the ecstasy of unfolding into awakening fully, every day, not just a few stolen hours between work and sleep. I want to taste the exquisite nectar of inner freedom, the gift of being myself.

In my twenties, I believed the path to success was going to a good school, getting married, having a family, and working (for someone else). I was highly ambitious and also profoundly lacking in confidence. Likely because of this lack of confidence, I was driven to succeed in my chosen field, which was art. I studied the CVs of successful artists who were making a name for themselves, and researched the best schools. I made a plan for my future success, and then I implemented it. Art was my shining star. Anything that got in the way of my success had no place in my existence. I knew who I was and what I was here to do. Getting my BFA and then going to graduate school to teach art at the university level was how I would share my voice with the world.

Despite not having a penny to my name, I enrolled myself in a highly prestigious private art school that costs more than $30,000 a year to attend. I was fortunate and also privileged. I received scholarships and had significant help from my family to make my dream a reality. I hated going into debt for my education, but felt committed to my vision of success. The relentless pressure to excel academically left me riddled with anxiety and in a constant state of fight or flight. I battled daily panic attacks for two and a half years. I wanted to quit school every day of those last two years of my program. Still, I remained committed to completing school as the path to my future success. Every day I woke up and did what I hated so that, eventually, I could have the freedom to do what I loved. I was committed to my success at all costs, even at the expense of my physical and mental health. I knew the way I was living made me miserable, but I did what I thought I needed to in order to live my dream. I wanted a life that felt free, and I was willing to sacrifice my every waking hour to get to that freedom. Looking back, I have so much compassion for that younger Mariko. I wish I had known that what I was seeking was my own self-worth and self-love.

After graduation, I had a spiritual awakening that looked like being stuck in bed for a year with adrenal fatigue. I moved to the West Coast and started to heal my body, studying energy healing, yoga, and somatic breathwork. I got my coaching certification and practiced more yoga. One day, out of frustration, I hired my first business mentor for $800. I was broke with a struggling energy healing business, so it was a significant investment. When I fell in love with marketing and the world of online business, I had a new vision for my success. I wanted to help people with the same things I was struggling with, living a life of freedom and finding love. I was studying online marketing by day and coaching my butt off at night. I went to coaching intensives and did hundreds of hours of mindset work and somatic healing. I hired high quality support from coaches, mentors and business strategists, wanting to reach that oh, so elusive, yet tantalizing place called consistent clients in my business—AKA cashflow positive!

It was overwhelming. I was doing all the things, but I felt blocked from my success. No matter what I did, I couldn't seem to get to my next level of income or find a loving partner I could claim forever. Frustrated with not having the success I ached for and feeling alone, I would sink into repeated cycles of excitement about the world of online marketing and periods of heavy burnout. I was drowning in endless workaholism to avoid feeling my sadness, trapped between brief moments of embodiment and my own out-of-control, wounded masculinity. When the clients and cash flow continued to dance before me, just out of reach, I started working longer and longer hours. I ignored my health and let my yoga practice drop off. I forgot to eat. I was continually in learning mode without ever graduating to the fun, money-making part. My days and nights were consumed with taking another course or watching another free training on marketing, sales, or client attraction. I wrote and published articles about embodiment, but I bounced between overwhelm and burnout in my daily practice.

Money was a constant source of anxiety. I had invested heavily into growing my business, spending tens of thousands of dollars on more coaching or hiring my next mentor, my checking accounts hovering continually on the edge of disaster. The expansiveness of time that I had felt when I was in my early twenties was melting away. I was alone without a partner. My business was far from stable, and I had nothing tangible to show for being in business except for my skills as a coach and a killer new MM LaFleur wardrobe.

I felt a deep sense of failure.

My dreams of having a loving partner and family and hitting consistent 10k months all felt frustratingly unavailable to me. I felt stuck. I knew parts of myself still needed healing. Something deep inside me was preventing me from having it all. At this point, I had been on my own healing journey for almost ten years. I meditated and did breathwork daily. I facilitated powerful workshops, and my clients had deep healings from my work. I knew that I was helping people and changing lives, sometimes in a single session, yet I couldn't seem to crack my own code for happiness and success.

I took a risk and hired one more mentor. The full price of her program was well outside my ability to pay, but I knew this teacher was for me. I applied for a partial scholarship and was accepted. The training was infused with Ayurveda and business magic. What I learned in this training gave me the push I needed to begin owning my voice and showing up as an expert in the online space. As a result of this mentorship, I got booked on podcasts and committed to sharing my work with Human Design. It was hard, but I committed to myself to become the expert I wanted to be. Slowly, one step at a time, I started to live into that future.

Then I hired another mentor who I adore. That investment in myself pushed all of my limits around money to their limits! This mentor lovingly but firmly held my hand as I walked into my fears around money scarcity and lack. She truly challenged me to step out of the toxic patterns I had created for myself and instead to trust and surrender, by letting go and not pushing so hard. She challenged me to spend at least one hour outside every day away from my work. At the time, it felt impossible to let go of control. I was working so hard and making so little money to show for it. Work was my unhealthy addiction, as was the time spent staring at my screen. I needed to unplug and reconnect with my body. I started going to the park every day to write and be with my thoughts.

And just like that, everything changed. When I allowed myself to surrender and not work so hard all the time, I met my dream person.

Laying in bed one night with my sweetheart, I checked my email and almost screamed when I saw a new $2,000 payment notification on my phone. I was in love *and* had just had the highest cash month in my business ever. I was expanding into my leadership and taking up space, stepping into my voice, no small feat for someone whose earliest memories involved shyness.

My business was ready to pop, and everyone could feel it, including my clients. I was doing more public speaking and new clients began finding me from those speaking opportunities. It felt like the hard work and daily actions were starting to snowball. And the best part was that my new success was magnetic. Everyone around me was riding the same wave. My clients were all breaking through glass ceilings left and right. I celebrated as they had their first successful 8k launch, created their first clients, or filmed video content while cross country skiing. I was a proud mama bear, and we were all so on fire.

Then, my relationship with my beautiful soulmate partner ended unexpectedly.

Time stopped. The world stopped for me.

I couldn't work. I had no desire for it, but even if I had, my computer was away in the shop being repaired for what felt like months. For weeks, a dull ache filled my stomach. I cried every day. The thought of letting go of this love felt unbearable, and the possibility of ever loving someone new offered no comfort. Gradually, like the lobster who doesn't realize she is being boiled alive, the dull ache in my stomach got worse and started to flash like a warning sign. After months in pain, I could avoid the physical signs no longer. For the first time in four years, I took my busy startup butt to go see a doctor. Feeling terrified of what he might say, I wore my favorite wool crepe MM blazer in a lovely shade of boss b*tch Capricorn grey. Whatever the bad news was, I wanted to look professional and put-together. Later, I sat in my car for hours sobbing.

The pain in my gut was apparently not just stress from my relationship ending. Based on what was going on with my body, I was told that I likely had Crohn's or ulcerative colitis. I hardly even know what these things meant. I felt such a strange mix of emotions and panic, and some distant part of me felt relief. Relief because for years, I had felt subtly that something was off in my body. Perhaps more tests would help me finally understand why I had felt so mysteriously ill for most of my life.

The timing of my illness was impeccable. I had just started a new eight week launch and was hoping to bring in $15,000 over the next seven weeks. I could feel my dream for the new launch falling back into the earth. I sat with my truth at this moment. My heart and body needed me to take a step back from my business to be present. I decided to cancel my launch and focus on my healing.

I stopped eating wheat and dairy, and I made myself a hypnosis meditation to listen to every day. I think most people believe that hypnosis is exotic in some way. The truth is we have so much power to impact our physical wellbeing by using the power of the subconscious mind.

The end of my relationship made space for some new things in my world. I decided to work on my anxious-avoidant attachment pattern. I started a regular EFT tapping practice to help me create healthier attachments in the future. I became an EFT practitioner. I cleaned and cleared my space. I learned about Astrogeography and North Nodes! I'd always looked down my nose at astrology. I cried a lot. I called my soul sisters. I changed what I ate. I held space for my mastermind clients and went for long walks by myself. I cooked beautiful food and worked on my capsule wardrobe, adding some touches of red to the blacks and creams. I bought a pair of red boots that I had seen in a dream years before the summer I lived in Baltimore when I walked my dog and wrote poetry.

Years ago, I took a workshop with a teacher named Paulus Berensohn. Paulus, the dancer, the potter, the shaman. I remember he once said: "I don't always know where I'm going, but a light comes on over where I'm supposed to move my hand next."

Through my long healing journey I finally came home to myself. For the first time I can remember, I feel truly whole, sovereign, and complete. I now love the work that I do as a coach. Looking back I see clearly how so much of my past pain has powerfully supported me in becoming a fearlessly empowered leader and the CEO of my own life.

On the outside, my success code has looked like many failures. At times there have been deep frustrations, lying in tears at the bottom of my closet. My success has looked like social media posts that nobody read. My recipe for slow unsexy success has looked like showing up and staying open and vulnerable in the possibility of rejection. It has been an unwavering commitment to my brand and my vision, always taking tiny steps but moving ever closer to who I am becoming. At times, success has been saying yes before I felt 100 percent ready and letting myself learn and be messy along the way— even during those moments when I didn't feel fully enough. Success means learning to expand beyond my own beliefs of what is possible and having the right tools to change my reality. My success has been learning to use my voice and being open to love.

Success is simply the ability to make money doing what you love.

Hey Next-Level Leaders,

I know what it's like to struggle with growing an online business. When I started my coaching business, I had my skills as a coach and a dream to create freedom working from my laptop. However, I had no clue how to market myself online, grow a following on social media or leverage my gifts into a profitable online business!

It is my joy and privilege to guide leaders like you to stand in your full power and fearlessly share your voice with the world. Hint: When you own your power and share your voice, everyone wins!

Now, two years into my online business, I have a job and a lifestyle I absolutely love. I am so glad I didn't give up on my vision. I feel tremendous gratitude that I get to wake up every day, without an alarm and do work I absolutely love, working with incredible clients just like you. Being the boss and CEO of my time is a dream come true. I now use my skills as a marketing genius to coach aspiring leaders like you to use your voice and to stand out and be seen online.

As a biz and leadership coach, I love supporting my clients in doing all the outer work of learning online business strategy, while also doing the emotional mastery and deep inner work of releasing the four biggest biz killers:

- Perfectionism
- Overwhelm
- Fear of being seen
- Burnout

If you're currently experiencing any of these right now, I'm here for you, because it is my joy and privilege to work with exceptional leaders, coaches, and creative entrepreneurs like you to get incredible results in your MAGNETIC business.

Now, more than ever, the world needs *you* to be unapologetically *YOU!*

ABOUT THE AUTHOR

MARIKO BRENNER

Mariko Brenner helps ambitious entrepreneurs carve a new path to success. As CEO and founder of Modern Muse, her mission is to help aspiring entrepreneurs increase their impact and income while having fun and inspiring global change. Her writing has appeared in Inspired Coach Magazine and The Collected Works of Poetry Pregame Volume One. In 2016, she founded the writing group Untitled, now known as the Sexy Writers Club. She looks forward to being published in two multi-authored books this year: Chyper and Success Codes.

Website: www.marikobrenner.com
Instagram: www.instagram.com/marikobrenner
Facebook: www.facebook.com/hypnosisbymm
Youtube: https://www.youtube.com/
channel/UCWLlfQf7jLRojkZeojx7sCQ
School: https://mariko-brenner-.teachable.com
Email: marikobrenner@gmail.com

17

NATALIE LOWRY

MY ROAD TO SUCCESS WAS A FOUR ACT PLAY

I think of my journey to success as a four-act play. Act One laid the groundwork for the path that was set forth for me by the expectations imposed by my family and society. Act Two established the trials and tribulations of my pursuit of success and the struggles that ensued. Act Three was when I began to realize my true potential, and recognized that I was meant to break free from the mainstream path. And Act Four was when I released what had been holding me back and embraced the world of opportunities that laid before me. *And the curtain rises...*

ACT ONE

I am a first generation Haitian-American. At a very young age, my parents' versions of success were instilled into my sisters and I. It was a requirement to excel in school and earn good grades. The ultimate vision of success in our household was to have a college degree, a well-paying job, a new home, a nice car, and plenty of money in savings. Nothing outside of this criteria would be considered success. With this ideal ingrained in my mind, almost every decision I made was in the pursuit of meeting these standards. As a senior in high school, my ten-year plan went as follows:

1. Graduate high school at 17

2. Get a Bachelor's Degree in Nursing by 21

3. Become a travel nurse (because they make better salaries)

4. Buy a house and a BMW by 23

5. Married by 24

6. At least 2 kids by 27

These were milestones I wanted to achieve to not only make my parents happy, but because I truly thought I wanted these things for myself. It took me a very long time to realize that I had been programmed to chase these dreams.

When I was seventeen, I started working for a major retail pharmacy with the intent of it being a short-term opportunity. The following year my parents decided not only to divorce, but to also sell the house we were living in. I immediately had to find a place of my own and support myself, and press pause on my college endeavors. My goals shifted and it became inevitable that my short-term job now became my long-term career as I no longer had the financial support of my parents. While steps 1-3 of the plan changed, I still believed that if I worked hard, moved up within the company, and made more money, I could support the lifestyle I dreamed of.

With goals of store management at the forefront, I was much closer to a salaried position, pension, and a secure retirement. Then the recession in 2009 hit, which led to changes in our company structuring. There would no longer be overtime, they would no longer offer pensions to long-term employees, the substantial bonuses that I looked forward to were a thing of the past, and they planned to eliminate many positions.

Even still, as I was chasing dreams that were not mine, there was even less reason to. I worked towards a college degree, even though I had no idea what specialization I wanted or what career I wanted it for. And despite being unhappy in retail, I continued to pursue this path reflexively. I was tired of all the setbacks thrown my way academically and professionally—and in hindsight it was because I was pursuing a path I never wanted.

I spent a great deal of time comparing my accomplishments, or lack thereof, to everyone around me. Between my quest to achieve the goals of others, and comparisons to others that I was making, I was miserable. I was racing to a finish line in a race where I didn't know the course. This led me spiraling into debt, depression, shame, embarrassment, envy, and hopelessness.

ACT TWO

All of these situations left me feeling depleted and alone. It seemed like everyone else around me had it figured out. So many of my friends and family were in committed relationships; some had kids, new homes, nice cars, college degrees, great jobs, they were well-traveled, and here I was in debt, not achieving any of my goals, single, childless, in living arrangements I was not happy with, and working a job I hated. Almost every step on my road to success was an obstacle. I felt like bad luck was my lot in life. Everyone around me was "successful", and at every turn I felt like I was a failure.

I remember talking to a fellow colleague who was a store manager before I became one myself. He had a side gig in real estate and I could not understand why someone making a salary like him would put so much effort into another part-time job. He told me it was his passion. He said he hoped to pursue real estate full-time and leave the company. I thought he was crazy for wanting to leave a stable and secure job for a "passion" where he could potentially make less money. At the time, I still believed that money equaled success and happiness. He shared that he recognized the risks, but believed that when you are doing something you love, the money will come. He asked what I was passionate about and I shared that my only passions were food, traveling, and watching tv, but knew that none of those things would pay my bills. We both laughed, but I was serious; I wasn't passionate about anything, and I could not wrap my head around the idea of interests or passions being at the heart of one's livelihood. This conversation stuck with me for years.

At that point I believed that passion was a luxury of people that had the help of parents to fall back on. When I thought of people pursuing their passions, I thought of struggling artists living in New York City: playing their music, sharing their mixtapes, displaying their art hoping to be noticed or maybe discovered. This is not the life I saw for myself, nor did it meet the criteria of any plan I had.

Once I was promoted to store manager, I thought I had finally proved myself worthy and successful. I had personalized business cards, my name was on the door of a store, and I was salaried. I was proud to share that I was a store manager because I thought it was an important title. It was not until after I left the company that I realized how meaningless it all was.

ACT THREE

Fast forward to the year 2018. I was fifteen years into my career and I had finally reached the end of my rope. I also had yet to complete my degree that was nine years in the making because of problems with the university I had attended. I was overwhelmed and unhappy. My company started increasing my workload and work hours, but not my salary. More major structural changes within the company led to the elimination of more positions, and many of my high-performing peers were losing their jobs. I felt my time was coming. I was scared and trapped since I had spent such a huge portion of my life in this business. Feeling completely helpless, I turned to psychotherapy to help me through my all-time low. It was one of the best decisions I made for my mental health and growth.

Therapy was exactly what I needed for a reprieve from my mental anguish. My therapist recommended many excellent resources for me to try, including yoga. I had thought to myself, "Me? Yoga?" I was not flexible, not skinny, and did not own "yoga attire". I had tried out yoga at a gym once and didn't get anything from it. It wasn't until my mother-in-law mentioned she wanted to check out a yoga studio nearby that I tried it again. I jumped at the offer since the first class was free and I ended up loving it. I signed up for a membership the next day and soon my one class a night routine turned into two classes, and then into three classes per day.

I was like a kid waiting for the school bell to ring waiting to leave work each day. I looked forward to yoga more than anything. I remember coming home to Will, my then boyfriend/now husband, and telling him how much I loved yoga and wondered if I had finally found my passion. This had me thinking of the conversation of years prior with my former colleague.

I was interested in deepening my practice and wanted to learn more. Soon after starting yoga, I also discovered Reiki Energy Healing. My new hobbies changed my evenings from winding down with a beer and complaining about how much my life sucked, to evenings filled with healing gatherings, women's circles, and reiki shares. I started to learn that there was more to my life than work, money, and status. I started to meet people that had left their conventional lives for something off the beaten path, and I wanted in!

I had concluded that yoga was my passion and I signed up for a 200-hour Yoga Teacher Training. Before the course even started, I decided that I wanted out of my career and to start a new life as a yoga teacher. I wanted the feeling I felt after class to be my entire life; to walk on clouds every day. I wanted to be relaxed and enjoy the company of people again; I wanted to be happy. This was my new idea of success.

Most of my friends and family were concerned about this crazy leap from a salaried job that had "benefits" to becoming a yoga teacher. I had to convince them of how desperate my plight was. I would explain how I struggled to get out of bed every day, to then sit in traffic for over an hour and a half, only to be miserable for a nine-hour shift, to then spend another hour and half back in traffic, inevitably coming home drained and defeated every night. I would count down the time to each vacation, but would not even enjoy my time off because I would count down the days until I had to return back to my dreadful job.

I was afraid to make a change—and so the universe made the move for me. In October 2018, I was put on a performance improvement plan by my boss which was their way of starting the process to get rid of me. I was terminated in May 2019. My boss asked me to meet him on a Friday, and I drove to my district office to hear those last parting words. After leaving my meeting with him and a woman from HR, I could not contain my smile as I skipped down the stairs and raced back to my car. I was free!

I was reluctant at first to share with acquaintances that I had been fired, so I would tell people I quit. But, I have since proudly corrected the narrative of my termination to being fired, because regardless of how it ended, it afforded me a new beginning to something much greater. It needed to happen this way, otherwise I would have never left. I soon began to describe my life as "Before Yoga" and "After Yoga" since finding yoga completely changed everything.

ACT 4

At first, I settled with the idea of just being a yoga teacher, working at a yoga studio, and eventually owning a studio. I briefly worked at a yoga studio teaching classes and managed their backend operations. When I outgrew this space, I took some time to figure out my next step. Once I committed to my personal growth, it became easier to invest in myself and envision my expansion. I have since completed various certifications, deepened my spiritual practices, and completed professional and personal development courses for my path in healing and wellness. The programs I have enrolled in have enriched my life in ways a college degree never could. I have released my personal limitations and pursued trainings in areas like Shamanic Healing and Birth Doula and continue to enjoy being a student of life.

In 2020, I launched my own business. I started meeting like-minded individuals in complementary fields that helped me build my brand. I have also worked with a few small businesses, utilizing the skills and structure I learned from my time in retail management, to help them grow and structure their own businesses. I have learned to harness my gifts and experiences in new ways to not only help myself, but to help others.

I have made my overall wellbeing a priority which has helped my mental, physical, and emotional health improve. I have also made a promise to myself to never enter a professional or personal situation where I feel my needs are not being met, or where I am not valued. I have become more attuned to how I feel and know when to honor my needs. While I am not making the same amount of money that I made in my retail career (yet!), I have my peace of mind, my health, I am much happier, and have learned to live with much less. I am also mindful of the fact that I have the potential to grow my business financially when I am ready, but also that there is no rush. In my time outside of the mainstream path, I have helped so many other people acknowledge their worth and the infinite possibilities that lie ahead of them. This is my vision of success embodied.

When I look back, I imagine how shocking it must be to people that have not seen or spoken to me in years; to remember who I was in my retail life and to see me now in my current path. And when revisiting my ten-year plan, it is evident that I did not achieve most of my goals, and the ones I did were not anywhere near the timeframe I had hoped for; regardless, my life is so much better in the new timeline I created.

I used to be down on myself for not attaining the same milestones as my peers, or I would be filled with regret and embarrassment over the "wrong" choices I made in my life. I spent a lot of time regretting my time in retail and thought it was a waste, but I have come to learn that all of the experience I gained while working in that career has helped me be successful pursuing my new professional endeavors and provided skills I can use going forward. There were no right or wrong decisions made; there were just choices. All of these choices have brought me to the life I am currently living, and I am happy where I am.

The last couple years have been so empowering to be surrounded by people that jumped off the mainstream track to take a chance on themselves and their passions. They continue to inspire me. I remember starting my life after yoga and meeting others that also felt trapped by their lifestyles and careers as well. They were burnt out and frustrated the same way I was but were too afraid to change their lifestyles or careers because they had children, or they were worried about what their families or spouses would think. I started to notice how so many people had been sold "the dream", but none of these dreams included happiness, overall well-being, or fulfillment. I wondered what the world would be like if this was a part of the planning for success?

The old mold that was previously set is no longer our reality. The workforce and many industry standards have changed drastically in the last twenty years. Many jobs no longer offer the stability of a thirty or forty year career. And the average person will change their career five to seven times in their lifetime, so why are we still encouraging people to stay on one path—and the same path as everyone else?

My mission has been to help others realize that there is a world outside of the conventional path. I want to help others to see that the social norms that have kept us boxed in for so many generations are what is holding us back from reaching our true potential. I hope that by living in my truth, others can feel empowered to challenge social norms and embark on a path that is aligned for them. Success is not linear; rather, it is more of a spirograph design. A linear trajectory is limiting since there is only one path and the outliers never make the final cut, whereas in a spirograph design, you can create your own path and the opportunities and outcomes are limitless. Success isn't just one thing or one way. Sometimes we'll be ahead and sometimes we'll be behind and that's okay. It's all a part of the experience.

Ultimately, meaningful success is going to look different for everyone. It can only truly be measured by each individual setting their own values independent of excessive influence from others. By the time this book is published, I will have birthed my first child. And as I reflect upon this, I wonder, what views will be imprinted onto them in regards to success? Will they see the experiences I went through and shape their own path without too much pressure from the outside world? I certainly hope so, but I know only time will tell. My hope is that whether you have already found your version of success or are still seeking it out, that you find peace and happiness while continuing to grow and redefine your own vision.

ABOUT THE AUTHOR

NATALIE LOWRY

Natalie Lowry is the owner and founder of Yemaya Yoga & Wellness. After starting a journey through yoga, and driven by her desire to carve out a new path for herself, Natalie decided to leave her career in retail management after sixteen years. She pursued trainings in Hatha Yoga, Aerial Yoga, Reiki, Birth Doula, and Shamanic Healing. Through these experiences and her passion for helping others, she uses her gifts to guide others to help shape their own vision of success, peace, and happiness. Natalie has helped empower nearly 100 women to define and achieve their own life goals while becoming champions of their own wellness. Natalie currently lives in New Jersey with her husband, Will and dog, Bella.

Website: www.yemayayogaandwellness.com
Instagram: www.instagram.com/natalied.doesyoga
Facebook: www.facebook.com/yemayayogaandwellness
Email: yemayayogaandwellness@gmail.com

18

POONAM MANDALIA

THE LIONESS ROARS

The beating of the heart resides
In the sound of the Lioness's voice.
She nurtures her tribe with loyalty,
Her life to fulfil and to rejoice.

She seeks to build to thrive.
Her hunt is in her wild nature,
Her wide brownish eyes.
Her Guardian Guide,
Her instincts shall continue to carry her,
Upon the heart path that she shall but only rely.

When intuition is lost in the world,
Does worry and pain create a danger and demise.
The joy in the heart is allowing,
Your life not to be built upon fictitious games and lies.

Success is a notion of saturation,
When society creates competition for recognition,
Built upon farce appearance through surface,

Defaced.
True blessing and miracle exist multidimensionally,
Within;
The deepest core that you see,
The Spirit inside that you breathe,
Inside all,
The Cosmos is laced.

When a Lioness roars,
She creates a web.
A resounding of love that is a great fire.
Fire is the flame found in your passions,
The passions built upon the truest and purest forms,
Destined forms of synchronistical sign,
Devotional dreams,
The Soul's Calling,
The deepest desire.

Expectations lose the hunt,
Intentions create the most magical maze.
Anger that is left untethered,
Leaves scars of wrath, leaking rage and remains.
Resentment carries a worrisome weight,
The Ego stops carrying the candlelit brightness of flame.

Forgiveness is the lightness,
That shines a beauty to all things,
The power that we can all use,
To allow vision.
To rebirth,
To co-create.

Compassion creates a virtue,
Of seeing how all things can generously relate.

Gratitude offers a Bumble-Bee humbling,
A life of heart-filled experience,
An alchemised abundance,
And,
That of caring grace.

Words are not the same as actions.
Angst actions match the infamous rat race.
Time is an illusion.
Our magnificence is what we must face.

We have the power to heal ourselves.
Yes,
We have the power to heal ourselves.
Grounding our paws to the ground.

Yes,
If only you could see your reflection,
Through the infinite mirrored halls of life.
Your sacred loops of ascension,
Would keep repeating,
Seeing a reflection profound.

Life is full of battle,
When we feel all is happening to us.
Life feels so precious to be lived,
When we take responsibility for all that we are able to give.

Life is not meant to be difficult,
Pain and suffering is a must.
There exists a polarity,
So that we learn,
Rewind,
Unwind,
And see that there is no such thing as loss nor a rush.

Love is free.
Life is bountiful when we are with trust.
Nothing can cause your destruction,
We were made to experience bliss,
We have been asleep and so we just simply forgot.

When a Lioness awakens,
Does she see the horizons before her.
True strength lies in courage.
The courage to take leaps into unknown territories,
To open our eyes,
To break comfort zones,
And to learn,
That we are worthy to receive the most tender and the most beautiful
love.

You are infinite,
You are change.
You are phenomenal,
You can live,
Success is the removal of all shame.

ABOUT THE AUTHOR

POONAM MANDALIA

Poonam Mandalia is a Medicine Woman, known by many names and many roles by those she works with. Shaman Poonam is a Master Shaman Teacher, Reiki Master, and Yogini. Her ancestral background as a fourth generational Psychic is deeply embedded in her work as a certified Womb Yoga Therapist and Classical Yoga Tantra Teacher. A Teacher of Psychic Healing Arts, Poonam trains Healers and initiates Priests and Priestesses into the advancement of their crafts of spiritual connection and intuitive channels.

Additionally, she is a Psychotherapist to many, providing therapy to heal core trauma wounds, depression, CPTSD, and grief. Her Medicine resides in her work as a Psychic Medium through the White Owl Spirit, as well as the Black Panthera; the Spirit Medicine of feminine consciousness.

Her brand and podcast are called *The Sacred Wombn*, because her life mission is to teach, create and nurture, much like the womb itself.

Website: https://www.thesacredwombn.com/
Instagram: https://www.instagram.com/thesacredwombn/
Instagram: https://www.instagram.com/thesacredwombn_podcast/
Podcast: https://thesacredwombn.buzzsprout.com/
Email: thesacredwombn@gmail.com

19

SIOBHÁN PHOENIX

SUCCESS MEANS RECONNECTING WITH OUR SOUL AS A PART OF A MULTIDIMENSIONAL UNIVERSE

*S*uccess is not a single aspect in a person's life, but it is deeply embedded in a person's entire way of being: it's in their way of thinking, the way of feeling and the way of acting.

We live in a strongly conditioned world. As soon as we are born, conditioning begins. We are simply being taught what is important in life and what is not. Important or unimportant from the point of view of society. A society in which most people have been taught these values since birth and incorporated them. We were not taught to think for ourselves and to decide for ourselves what is important for us, but we were taught to adopt the opinions of others.

Outdated social structures

What you think about success has a lot to do with what you were raised to think. For most people, success means following a traditional path, following footsteps that many people have followed before. They became a copy of someone else's idea of success. Yet this does not make anyone truly happy or sustainably successful.

Social structures are always developed in the same way: a courageous, innovative person develops a certain way of living that makes him feel satisfied. Other people admire this lifestyle and imitate it. For this pattern now to be socially recognized, a larger movement occurs and is often developed and spread through political or business attention. This attention happens when a new idea or way of life promises an economic upswing, such as the industrial revolution, when national economies boomed and business owners of production companies gained. It gave many people a regularly paid job. But it also led to a change in social processes and collective thinking. As soon as something is recognized and advertised politically, economically, or in the media, the collective often jumps on this new idea without considering whether it is good for them personally. In this way, people lose the connection to themselves and their desires—but this connection is essential for success in life!

We have lived like this for centuries, even millennia. The industrial revolution is just one example out of the nearest past. We follow the opinions that are imposed on us from outside. At the same time, this is the cause by which we have completely lost connection with our true selves, our inner being, our true dreams and desires. And it is also the root cause for losing our connection to all that is and to all living beings—be it humans, animals, or plants. We have learned to follow the beaten path instead of walking our own. We lost ourselves in society. And out of this lost place, we cannot create sustainable success or bear it from within.

A common association with the outside world's definition of success is money. Many live in fear of not having enough money to live on. But this thinking is a fallacy that makes you immobile when it comes to fulfilling your destiny, for which you were reincarnated on this planet. This fear keeps you stuck in old believe systems and unhealthy patterns. Money is an exchange of energy, and it is wrongly anchored in people's minds that it is only possible to make money by hard work. Mankind is so attuned to this idea that it must be hard to make money, that it has become difficult for them to stop suffering for it. People have locked themselves in their false beliefs.

They calibrated themselves to suffer and keep themselves from becoming the great people they can be while allowing the money to easily flow to them. I want to challenge you to become the amazing person you are meant to be. The money will automatically follow your energy!

Quantum leap

We all live in a quantum world in which everything is energetically connected. Humanity had long forgotten about this connection and lived apart from everything that is. The human mind created a new reality based on duality and lack of connection. Humanity separated into loneliness and forgot its energetic connection to everything in existence. And out of this separation, humanity tried to become successful. A low vibrating success that is attempted to be achieved through struggle and competition rather than enjoying the naturally high vibrational state of success that comes from pure connection to all that is.

We are now living in a time in which we can break through these established low frequency structures and find our way back to the real nature of our soul essence. We are allowed to reconnect with ourselves, with our wonderful planet earth and all its creatures, with the whole universe and all its dimensions and with everything beyond. We may understand that we are not separate from everything that is, but we are connected as a part of it. If we let this truth back into our lives and embed it in our work here on earth, we will have the greatest possible success. We will fulfill the purpose of our soul and we will not lack anything earthly that we need for life. We will make this planet the most beautiful it can be.

If you are someone who can relate to this, let your gut feeling answer the following questions:

- Do I want to be more in touch with myself?
- Is it my desire to regain my innate power?
- Do I want to live my life free from conditioning?

- Is it my desire to be more connected to life and its miracles?
- Do I want to live unapologetically?
- Is it my desire to live in true abundance?

It indeed is possible! I believe that you are more than ready for a journey into a new life, into a new era of being your own helmsman. In fact, I believe that this is the new way of living where humanity is heading. When I look back over the past decade, but especially the past one or two years, it seems like time is moving faster. Events come quickly and densely, and more and more people are asking themselves: What is really important to me? Times change quickly, patterns change quickly, and humanity is quickly steering towards a more aligned life with itself and with everything in existence. People are beginning to feel connected to all that is.

A new era

We need to look inward. Success is an inner job. We have to ask ourselves: "Who am I? And why am I here? How can I serve this planet with my gifts?" We as humans are not here by chance! We are here to fulfill our personal, unique destiny. Find out what this is and grow out of your conditioning. Do not let anyone distract you from being who you truly are. Courageously go your own way towards your destiny, strength, happiness, and success. When you align with your inner calling and your higher self, everything else follows automatically. To be successful, it is enough that we connect with ourselves and question what we have learned in the outside world about success and let go of this misunderstanding once and for all.

As humans, we have an innate creative power within us that wants to bring something on its own to the collective. This means that everyone on this planet has their own personal path to truly sustainable success and thus their own personal path to lasting happiness. Personally, I would even go so far as to say that our soul incarnated here on earth for a specific reason at this special time and in today's society. Our soul knows the best way for our life, and we just must listen and follow, and we will automatically be on track of our purpose here on earth. Our soul speaks to us as our intuition and is there all the time, no matter if we listen or not. The reason so many people on this planet are unhappy in their corporate jobs is because they have stopped listening to their intuition. We often do not look inside ourselves to find out our path in life, but instead look to someone else's. This leads us away from our purpose, our true happiness, our inner fulfillment, and our true success.

Called to fulfill my purpose

When I was a child, I always wondered why my parents kept telling me to always listen to them, my teachers in school, and basically everyone who they thought was a "good" adult. To me, adulthood did not mean that this person was wise or a natural authority just because of their biological age. I once tried to speak to my parents about my point of view, but they did not understand. They did not understand how I could think that all human beings are equal, and how I can think that even animals and plants should be included in that equality. There was no equality for them. They believed in the social hierarchy, and that I should too. They told me that I can see everywhere how well the rich are doing and how badly the poor are doing. Well, this explanation never convinced me because my parents spoke of money and superficial wealth, while I believed that people's outer life should always reflect spiritual equality. My parents laughed at how philosophical I was and asked where I picked it up. I could not remember picking it up anywhere. I just did not understand how to think in terms of social structures, nor why I had to learn certain behaviors.

Over the years, I have adapted to society and how it works, learning to live in a system that seemed deeply artificial to me and that I deeply rejected. But this adaptation helped me when I started working for a big corporation. At least, when it came to adapted, socially compatible behavior. Inwardly, I felt separated from myself and my personal truth. This separation between myself and my inner truth did not make me happy, no matter how high I climbed the corporate ladder and no matter how much money I earned. I withered inside like an unwatered plant, which made me sadder and sadder over the years up to a chronic depression and recurring burnout. I moved further and further from my true north, only to satisfy my surroundings, until luckily—or by fate—I experienced something very strange and, at the same time, deeply arousing.

I was sitting in a business meeting. Bored, unhappy and on the verge of the next burnout, my consciousness suddenly floated to the ceiling and looked down at my body. Then, I heard a voice speak to me. It sounded familiar, calm and wise: "This is not your life! Find your way back to yourself and to the reason why you incarnated here on earth!" And suddenly, the distance between my body and my consciousness at the ceiling seemed to be increasing rapidly. I saw my body as an increasingly tiny point from an ever greater distance.

Someone in the room asked me a business-related question, and I winced when I realized I was looking through my human eyes again at the same moment. I answered the question, but what I had experienced had a lasting effect. I took a few days off, and then quit my corporate job and left behind that lifestyle.

Now, I would not say I had an awakening. I was there and awake the whole time. However, I was hidden behind fear and the learned compulsion to adapt. Being myself did not seem safe. That was something I would be judged for, and for some reason, acceptance was particularly important to me. I did not dare to break out of that pattern from childhood and come into my full strength for a long time. Eventually, the out-of-body experience led me to the courage to take control of my life and follow my innate destiny.

Shifts

This happened in the summer of 2016. I have never regretted the decision to leave the traditional path and go my own way! But that does not mean it was easy. I did not turn my whole life around in just one day. I travelled through all the dark memories and belittling patterns and beliefs, and turned my whole life upside down and checked what still resonates with me and what does not. If you were born on this planet at this time, there are many processes to go through once you decide to go your own path. And no, I dare not say I am completely healed. In fact, I believe that no one on this planet is fully healed at this point of time. But we are on our way—and that is what matters.

On this journey, I realized that I also want to help other people to return to their true selves. To create a world of happiness, bliss and true success, everyone on this planet must reconnect to their true essence and live it. In this way, we will create a society of love, compassion, and cooperation. A connected society, connected with people, animals, plants, earth, and the universe. A society that understands how wonderful our connection with everything is and how deep and far it extends into other dimensions and timelines, as well as beyond.

For this reason, I have dived deep into spiritual teachings, quantum physics, energy healing, coaching techniques, yoga, meditation, breath work, and embodiment. To find the way back to ourselves, it is necessary to look deeply and heal even deeper. I combine all this knowledge for work with my clients to be able to help them on their way to themselves and their true north. It is not possible, for example, to heal only the mind. True deep healing requires healing of the emotions, the mind, the soul, and the body. Working on your entire energy system will even help you heal physical illnesses, as physical illnesses are only a symptom of a much deeper and often hidden cause.

Become a leader of the new Earth

I passionately believe that the time has come when more and more people realize that they no longer want to be locked into social norms and regulations. The time has come when more and more people want to free themselves from the ailing belief system and courageously go their own way.

My own voice now flowing into these words is based in a deep transformation that was a truly cathartic process leading me back to my spiritual roots. I wish you, and everyone on this planet, the willingness to jump into the deep transformation to yourself and your inner calling. I wish you and everyone on this planet the courage to take the necessary steps to reunite with yourself and your true essence. This is how you come to know great happiness and become successful in a truly unique and fulfilling way.

I believe that you reading these lines means you are aware of the separation humankind finds itself in and at least somewhat feel its friction against the true human nature. I believe you want to come back to our most natural way of living and long for a better world. That makes you one of the few people who already realized that our way of living is wrong, and that success defined by duality and separation is not sustainable. That makes you a leader, a leader towards a new, better world. A guide towards a connected humanity. A lighthouse of a new Earth. You reading this means that you are ready for big changes.

With all my infinite love for you,
Siobhán Phoenix

ABOUT THE AUTHOR

SIOBHÁN PHOENIX

Siobhán Phoenix is a certified life coach and energy healer, as well as a yoga, meditation and mindfulness teacher. She has more than 10 years of experience in the corporate world, leading international IT projects for some of the world's leading companies. Over the years, the desire to leave the corporate world grew stronger as did the desire to give life more meaning and make an impact in the world. In her work as a spiritual life coach and energy healer, she now helps her clients to reconnect to their heart and intuition and find their own way to success that is not defined by social conditioning and learned patterns. Siobhán helps her clients to find the courage to take necessary steps and changes in life to find more happiness, purpose, fulfillment, abundance and bliss. She combines coaching experience with energy healing, embodiment, movement, breath-work, meditation and yoga.

Websites: https://www.siobhanphoenix.com
https://www.findingbliss.com
Instagram: https://www.instagram.com/siobhan.phoenix
Facebook: https://www.facebook.com/Siobh%C3%A1n-Phoenix-Spiritual-Life-Coaching-and-Energy-Healing-104046305249286

20

SOFIYA MARIYA

WOMB ALCHEMY: YOUR PORTAL OF SUCCESS

*T*here is so much good that comes out of learning; knowledge is power after all. However, I have realized that the greatest lessons often come in the unlearning of all we know. The process of unprogramming the false stories and limitations that are superimposed upon us from the moment we are born is one of the most important experiences we can give ourselves. Discovering your unique success code comes in the unlearning of all the rules and restrictions you've been taught, and unearthing your passion to express yourself authentically in every aspect of your life.

The concept of success has been drowned in perfectionism, elitism, and privilege, and it has kept so many people feeling so small. Personal net worth as a measurement of success has created an association with emotional self worth as well, which in turn creates a self-sabotaging cycle as we compare ourselves to millionaires and consistently feel like we are not enough. This can lead to feelings of depression and anxiety, and it disconnects us from true internal and longstanding happiness.

It's rare that we are encouraged to decide for ourselves what success means to us. So, in this moment, ask yourself: what does success mean to you? Asking ourselves this question awakens us to the truth that we have the power to create our own version and measure of success, regardless of what we've been told is "right".

Growing up with young parents who immigrated to America from Ukraine strongly influenced my perception of success. Immigration molds you into a machine of fear and lack, while dangling an imagined "American Dream" in front of you as you suffer to make ends meet. The story was always "life is work, not fun". I remember embodying so much shame about being from a family of struggling immigrants; I felt like, because we weren't financially well off, we were worth less.

My internalization of the immigrant experience led to lying about where I lived, what I owned, and who I was — all so that I would feel like I was worthy of having friends at school, and out of a wanting to be liked. From a young age, I felt that my worth was measured by money and external validation, which created an unhealthy habit of anxious perfectionism from age six. Perfectionism very quickly became a way for me to control life around me, creating scenarios where I could prove I was worthy of love and external validation, and therefore money and success. This is a theme easily seen in adulthood today, as people grind through long work hours, give up time with family, get almost no vacation days, all so that we can prove to society and to ourselves that we are worthy of money and success.

Like all things in this world, the concept of success is evolving. Why are we still basing success on the broken scale of society, giving away all our power to a machine that keeps us in a state of survival rather than uplifting us to thrive? It is up to us, individually and collectively, to unlearn this false limiting belief that is a byproduct of suffering generations, and to rewrite our story of what success is. And we know that success is not a "one size fits all" label that anyone can put on and receive the same outcome. Success is a unique personalized experience of creation, moving through us and out into the world.

When I was growing up, my parents decided I should become a dentist. Most of my family on my mom's side were dentists. It was a job that fit a formula of having a secure income. Yet it never clicked for me. When at eighteen I said no to my parent's dreams of me becoming a dentist, I said no to an experience of success that I knew was not for me. In a society where we are not encouraged to explore the depths of our soul and what truly makes us happy, at eighteen years old, somehow I still had to trust my internal feeling for when to say no. I remember lying in bed crying at the thought of working a job I couldn't stand for the rest of my life. It felt soul-crushing. Around the same time, I also began to divert away from the Catholic Church I had been raised in to explore spirituality and the concept of self-empowerment. I followed my passion for healing, and was led to mentors, healers, ceremonies and initiations all over the world. I knew it was my soul's purpose to help others, but I first had to unlearn many layers of limiting programming that were keeping me feeling small, afraid, and powerless.

Discovering the realm of self-healing changed my life. I began to feel so alive and inspired, and totally surrendered to this inner compass of truth within me. When you trust the divine within you, you are led to magical people and places. In this trust and surrender, I have been able to travel to twenty-five countries and experience life-changing moments around the globe: working with plant medicine shamans in South America, hiking up sacred mountains barefoot, and facilitating ceremonies at sacred portals such as the pyramids of Egypt, Stonehenge, Machu Picchu, the pyramids of Mexico. I knew that in order to create the life I desired, I had to be the one behind the wheel: not the fear and lack that I had been programmed to exist in. Along with traveling, I would dive headfirst into any new experience that life presented to me, like hula hooping with fire, selling upcycled clothing at festivals, being initiated into the Magdalene Rose Mystery School, and starting my own healing business. I followed my passion, and it continuously led me home into my body and soul. Each of these experiences offered me an opportunity to redefine success from what my parents wanted to instead following my passions and cultivating deep happiness and self-love.

Throughout these years of self-empowerment and discovering who I am, I have been so drawn to the womb as a portal for all of the growth and healing I experienced. It felt like I could speak another language. I could hear the whispers of my true self directing me towards experiences that would further activate the codes of success and empowerment within me. The womb presented itself as a golden gateway for me to step through to access all parts of myself: my inner child, my ancestral karma, energy of past lovers, my mindset, my relationship with my body and pleasure, my shadow self — the list goes on and on. I quickly learned that in order to create the life I desired, I first had to rebuild the reality that exists within me. Your internal reality mirrors outwardly to your external. The cultivation of your internal reality is the only way to create long standing happiness, as your emotional state is nurtured by self-love rather than ruled by external experiences. The more I released old wounds and trauma, the more I was able to tap into my creative life force.

To clarify any limiting misconceptions of the womb, here it is; an energetic space within your sacral area that is the epicenter of your body's life force energy. It is the motherboard of all the life force energy within you, and the state of your womb can determine the state and quality of your life. The womb is the portal of all your creative energy, and it carries the codes for all that you seek to create. Everyone has an energetic womb portal.

The creative life force within my womb unveiled my divine purpose to me, teaching me that I am destined to help women heal their wombs and midwife the rebirth of the Divine Feminine on our planet. The continuous surrender to my passions and my truth is what has led me to being twenty-seven and running two healing businesses. This is an external measure of success that is a culmination of over ten years of healing, growth, and following my truth even when it was really hard. The journey of redefining success has been challenging, and it's also been the most rewarding way to live. So many of us are alive, yet so few of us are actually living. My personal success codes have activated me to be a part of the mission that helps others actually thrive rather than just survive. We have forgotten that we are the Master Creators of our reality, and it's time we remember.

Success is a journey of becoming who you truly are and cultivating happiness along the way. This is a new and redefined perspective of success that I have intentionally chosen as my truth. Success as a measurement of worth in society that's based on your income or material items is a self-sabotaging hamster wheel that keeps you spinning in circles. repeating the same patterns, and coming from a place of not feeling like you're enough. These patterns based on lack make you play it safe and hold you back from taking leaps of faith and trusting in your power to create. Success is the shift we make from victim to empowered one as we reclaim our ability to transmute our pain into power. The womb is the portal of this transmutation. It's the gateway into your truth that is waiting to be revealed and embodied.

To be guided back into your womb as a portal for success is to be led into a safe haven of truth and intuitive guidance. The womb works in tandem with your heart as your internal navigation system that directs you towards a reality built on authentic self-expression. This type of reality liberates you from societal expectations and broken measures of success, because rather than being built on fear and lack, it is built on trust and self-love. As the Master Creators of our reality, we build our empire upon solid ground that can firmly support all that we create. As the queen of my own personal empire—my reality —I am the one in power who gets to decide what is and is not success. This is where we must tune into our truth that swims within the waters of our womb, and infuse this truth into the empowered action that we take towards a happy and healthy lifestyle. It's a sacred dance of the Divine Feminine and Masculine that keeps us centered and in alignment with our Divine purpose.

The power of Divine purpose has no numerical value. It's a unique essence we all carry within ourselves. My Divine purpose is to help women reclaim their womb as a portal of creation and transform their pain into power. The womb is the portal to success—a sacred space containing your creative life force that yearns to be harnessed with loving intention and channeled into the external world. This alchemical process of creation is the driving force merging you with your dreams. It inspires you to be of service in whatever way resonates with you on a soul level. There are no wrong answers. Through womb work, I have helped hundreds of women discover their unique divine purpose by reuniting them with their True Self.

We all have our personal codes of success that are expressed through us in all that we do. Gone are the days when success was measured by the money in your bank account, or by the number on the scale, or by the type of car you own. These are all materialistic things that provide short-term external validation and happiness. Success is based on the state of your internal reality first: your relationship with yourself and your connection to living your life. Success is about releasing expectations of perfectionism and embracing the fluctuating messiness of life. Success is about saying yes to the ideas that are seeded in your consciousness that make your heart flutter every time you think of them as a reality. The first step to success is self-love, where the womb is the gateway into all aspects of the self and where the deepest levels of healing and growth occur. It's in this growth that you realize the power you hold to create your life based on your passions and truth. This realization single-handedly activates the codes of success within you at a soul level, infusing your unique essence into all the creations that are birthed through you.

All the answers you seek are already within you, residing deep within your womb. It is there for you to call upon every day and at any moment you need guidance and support. By accessing this internal support system, you are tapping into the flow of creation and aligning yourself with your divine purpose. This is the process of activating the Divine Feminine within you, and giving her space to intuitively lead you to all that you are meant to create and experience. Miracles cannot be calculated or planned; they happen when we are in the flow and in tune with our natural rhythm of life. By surrendering to the wisdom of your womb, you are stepping into trust. This actively sends out a signal to the Universe that you are ready for all the blessings and abundance that can only be provided for you when you are living as the embodied version of your true self. Your true self is revealed layer by layer, as you release attachments to limiting beliefs and stories that have kept you interpreting reality through a lens of fear and lack. Womb alchemy is the process of awakening from living in fear, as you remember your truth, your passion, and your power.

It is time for you to reclaim success as an essence of fulfillment and embodiment rather than a number. That essence is first and foremost cultivated within, through reclaiming your relationship with yourself and life and choosing to align your life with your truth. Your truth is the message of your soul; it whispers of heart aligned desires and expansive realities that give you opportunities to share your true self with the world. Whether those opportunities are expressed through experiences of writing a book, having a family, being dedicated to your mental health, or having a multimillion dollar business, it's *all* an expression of success. Your expression of success is unique to your personal desires, to the codes within your soul, and the individualized magic that you embody. Your essence of success resides within your womb, pulsating with life and ready to be born.

ABOUT THE AUTHOR

SOFIYA MARIYA

Sofiya Mariya is the Creatrix of Womb Alchemy, a licensed acupuncturist, and a priestess of the Magdala Rose Mystery School. Her Womb Alchemy coaching business is dedicated to helping women reclaim their womb as their sacred portal of creation by transforming their pain into power. She weaves wisdom from many traditions to create a deep life-changing experience for her clients. Sofiya works deeply with Divine Feminine energies and has supported hundreds of women through coaching, women's circles, retreats, and energy healing. She is fiercely dedicated to helping women embody their true and most empowered self. Sofiya has been a guest on podcasts such as *Soul Elixir* and *Green Queen,* hosted by Miss Europe 2018's Luissa Burton. She has traveled the world to study with healers, shamans, and priestesses, learning how to work with energetics to promote individual and collective healing.

Website: www.WombAlchemy.love
Instagram: https://www.instagram.com/sofiyamariya_wombalchemist
Facebook: Womb Alchemy
Email: sofiya@wombalchemy.love

21

STEPHANIE C KOEHLER

FROM FEAR TO FIERCE: FORGING YOUR OWN TRUE PATH TO BECOMING UNAPOLOGETICALLY YOU

hen you truly step across the threshold to becoming ALL of YOU, you will start breaking free from any and all misconceptions around success. When you innerstand that we have been fed lies and been programmed to 'function' in societies that do not hold your highest interest in mind nor promote a sense of self-realization, rather focus on the profit for an elite few, you can wholeheartedly step outside the confines of illusionary boundaries to forge your unique path.

We are shifting! As humanity, the Collective, and individually. This stepping through a gateway is also the moment when you realize that you do in fact have all the answers within, that you are not lacking anything and that it is YOU who is capable to create and live your Sacred Dream—or not—depending how much you desire to live in your highest expressions and how willing you are to take full responsibility for your life. All of it, all areas and aspects, at all times and circumstances! It is also the moment when you innerstand that any mentor, coach or program you sign up for is merely a doorway to Soul-remembrance and not meant to become someone other than you following your Soul's chosen journey. It is supportive of our accelerated growth and expansion with the aim to walk yourself home!

This path is not for the faint of heart but for those who know deep within their Soul that they chose to dedicate themselves to the work they are here to do. It is for those who know deep down that they committed to bring their purpose to fruition, unwavering and unafraid of what stands in the way. It takes dedication to stay the course, a willingness to surrender and trust in the mystery and a commitment to Self-Mastery, calling BS onto one's self whenever needed, fueling our own fire, and utilizing the tools we garnered along the path to vibe high. It takes an openness to let go of what does not serve us in the Highest and discernment not to get lost in the flurry of things along the way. And it also means taking soul-aligned actions that get you to where you desire to be. Not just once or twice with an expectation that your life will look radically different tomorrow, but daily, until you have become the master of navigating the field of energies, knowing that all happens in divine timing. Surrendering and trust are key components of this journey. Become the keen observer of your mind, thoughts, and all of your actions, and start co-creating with the Quantum field.

Working and co-creating with the Quantum field is not a lofty, unattainable fairy tale, it is a scientifically proven way through which you can rewire your nervous system, deprogram yourself from old stories, and start honing in on your gifts to live in higher vibrations. Tapping into the Quantum allows us to raise our frequencies to match that which we desire to bring into matter. And the more grounded and present we are, the higher we can rise. There is a balance to being able to tap into visioning your desired outcomes and feel them in most detail, while at the same time being so rooted that you are capable to bring those visions to fruition.

My innerstanding of frequencies and how energy works has evolved immensely over several years. At times I think I lived under a rock for most of my life, completely unaware of my Divinity and Soul's true expressions. I experienced a fair share of trauma in this lifetime and many prior ones that ranged from sexual, verbal and emotional abuse starting at a very young age, with a direct correlation into most of my adult intimate relationships to further traumatic experiences including my father's suicide when I was only seventeen years old. The childhood sexual molestation caused me to completely block out the experience and not revisit it until my early twenties. My father had already passed, and with that, I was spared the opportunity to confront him in his human form. I did, decades later, in communion with sacred plant medicine where I healed some remaining layers of this experience that had evolved around self-worth and self-love, and my ability to be fully emotionally available in my relationships.

In my mid-twenties, I moved to Spain to study linguistics, and soon after worked at a press agency. This eventually led me to living in the U.S. Overall it was an amazing journey of exciting opportunities and the deep satisfaction of traveling around the globe with many trials and tribulations. But it wasn't until later that I innerstood I had been trying to run away from myself all along. I had also been seeking validation and answers from outside myself, which left me with a sense of lack and a burning desire to simply get rid of any scars or feelings of anger and unworthiness. I bottled up my anger, which then reared its ugly head on many occasions as I had simply not learned how to express it in a healthy way. Rage can be an extraordinarily powerful emotion--energy in motion! It is just when we don't deal with it and give it any space to express what wants to be heard that it goes haywire and can cause quite a bit of damage.

I didn't innerstand then, and only connected many of the dots within the past years. But all of those experiences helped me to become the woman I am today: the fierce, compassionate, powerful Goddess that I am, the Light Keeper, the Earth custodian, medicine woman. Over several decades, I tried many modalities to heal from my trauma and regain a new perspective of wholeness. This was not easy and was definitely an ongoing process of learning and growing, innerstanding and expanding to the fact that we are already whole to begin with.

For many years after I first started seeking out psychotherapy, I shifted from feeling like a victim to a survivor. This felt aligned for a very long time, in which I also dedicated some years to work as a volunteer at a local Rape Crisis Center in California to emotionally support women and men whose rape had been reported through their law enforcement interrogation and forensic exams. Ultimately, I made a conscious choice to no longer stay held back by defining myself as a survivor, and rather declare that I was the creatress of my own reality. And, that I in fact was able to rewrite my story in whichever way I wanted.

This is when everything started to change. My mother's passing in July 2017 was the turning point in my life, where I just knew deep within my bones that there was more to life than hustling from paycheck to paycheck, with this relentless reminder popping up in my mind of not living my truth. Together with my brother, telling her that she would not win her battle with cancer and would pass was the hardest thing we ever did, and the memories of this moment still bring me to my knees today. Seeing her take her last breath about a week later was the most sacred I could have ever imagined. It was one where I fully innerstood the vastness of our Soul's Divinity. I know in my heart that she passed so that I could ultimately be free; she had taught me liberation in so many ways. Today, she is closer than ever, and she always makes herself known and sends messages. Her love is infinite. I dedicate this chapter to her as she was the one who always encouraged me to live my own true path, regardless that it meant causing her pain as I lived continents away from my family since my mid-twenties.

After her passing, I decided to radically let go of the life I had created for myself and pulled the ripcord to follow my Soul's calling and pursue my biggest dream to experience 150 countries before I turn ninety. On June 6, 2018, I left California, after I had sold, gifted or donated most all my belongings. The visceral pain I had felt for years of not living my truth had become greater than the fear of the unknown. My location independence started in Peru, diving into the world of sacred plant ceremonies and many more experiences around the world that left my heart and mind blown wide open. It was the gateway for me to expand my consciousness, to tap deeply into my Soul's human experience of becoming. It literally opened a new world for me.

What I know to be true is this: the only thing that stands between you and your most outrageous and wildest dream is YOU! Shed these illusions of lack and scarcity in your mind that have held you back from living your dream. When I got off the plane in Peru, I saw with my own eyes that I was not the only person on the planet exiting the matrix and pulling the ripcord to start a new chapter in life, freeing myself from the shackles. At that moment, I realized that I had crossed an invisible fence where on one side many people were stuck in their self-imposed cages and limiting beliefs, and on the other side I was met by those who forged their own path.

And to make it very clear, the distinction between the two has nothing to do with money. I have met a huge spectrum of humans and their way of living. Some are without a cent to their name, volunteering or somehow making their way through, while others are multi-millionaires living their dreams on their terms. Most are quite content with their journey. Whether or not you declare your sovereignty comes from a place of your Soul and your ultimate belief in being deserving of creating and living your sacred dream. This is something no one other than YOU can offer to you.

Have you ever noticed that some people just seem to attract everything and everyone? They carry a glow that is noticeable and ignites a sense of curiosity by the observer. What feels so magnetic is the Light that someone holds. Literally! Thriving in higher frequencies creates more photons (light) in our carbon-based bodies, and this is what appears to produce a glow. For example, looking at a scale of consciousness map, destructive energy like fear that causes anxiety and worry and is repelling is measured at 20 on this map. Compare this to love, which with its pure happiness and purity of motive, is very attractive in nature and is associated with a creative energy of 500 on the same scale. From there, it rises all the way up to enlightenment with Christ Consciousness frequencies of 700-1,000. Aiming to thrive high allows us to step fully into the gifts and talents we hold and receive to share in this lifetime. It also allows us to motivate and ignite others into their own version of the same.

As we strive to let go of old layers and step more and more into the Light—our Light!—with each layer of letting go, we are moving away from our carbon-based bodies and closer to a plasma-based vehicle where we shine as the luminous beings we truly are. This is where we experience Oneness and Divine Love, play, and joy, and access full Soul-remembrance. This is also often referred to as shifting from a 3rd dimensional reality by crossing the 4-D bridge, to eventually live in 5-D consciousness. What happens on this journey of transformation is a natural shedding of old programs, ancestral DNA imprints and false templates to hold and sustain the light in those higher dimensions where we also upload new codes and receive immense upgrades for our journey ahead. We detach from the physical vessel we have chosen for this linearity, released from the earthly material things we once defined ourselves by.

The process of shedding and purging is one of getting well, of feeling whole, of Soul remembrance, and not something to be feared, disregarded or spiritually bypassed. In order for lower emotions like anger, shame, and grief to be released, we have to make space for these emotions to be felt first to then transmute them into those of higher frequencies. How we do so is a choice and can absolutely happen with ease and grace. Now, this doesn't translate into these phases always being joyful. On the contrary, they might be felt as exhaustion, pain, a sense of loss of identity as we shed from our physical, emotional, and energetic bodies on a subatomic level. However, we can absolutely enter these waves of purging in a very mindful way.

Please note a word of caution for purging: there is a fine line between allowing oneself to enter into a purging process to peel another layer and let go of old programming to ascend further with an innerstanding that certain lessons needed to be learned, and on the other hand being addicted to purging and the navigation of your shadow self to a point where you reactivate old and create new stories of the same dense energy. The former is called Self-Mastery! Needless to say, we are infinite Souls in this human experience with free will. Which route you will take is up to you. Just know that either way, it is a choice!

We all hold gifts and talents that are unique to us, like coded medicine and sacred geometries through which we activate and ignite others on their path. It is so vital to innerstand that these gifts are not to be kept for self or hidden from the world. They are to be shared, widely!

In this age of Aquarius we just entered, we are all invited to stand tall and support one another to shine, to fully live in our true embodiment, and to co-create. Co-create with the Divine, co-create with others you meet along the path. We are moving away from the once Pisces-led attitude of "power over to power with". It is this innate innerstanding that, when we support one another in our unique gifts and offerings, everyone wins. And it also refers to the Universe holding and offering unlimited resources. There is no shortage in any way of any thing. Seeing these Universal principles play out before my eyes has been very empowering.

I am deeply grateful for the mentors I had and have today who have helped deepen my connection to Self and the Divine. And I am especially grateful for having finally surrendered fully into the mystery. It was that moment where I felt most at home, whole, loved, seen, and honored, and where every step along the way was a complete confirmation and lineup of synchronicities divinely led by Source. The guidance I received from my higher dimensional star family and guides is nothing short of miraculous and awe-inspiring.

Their way of nudging me to stay the course and meeting me halfway has been the most empowering experience to date. And it is from this place that I offer what I do. Full-heartedly and in trust that we are here to shine. Living a life of joyful abundance, optimal health, and divine love is our birthright. In fact, we ARE love, abundance, joy. Those are qualities of our Soul.

My work today is a weaving of quantum science with ancient wisdom traditions, which combines 5D activations with shamanic practices, rituals, coaching and Quantum modalities such as Quantum Healing and Quantum Flow. These practices help to release blockages and limiting beliefs, to embody one's gifts and live one's purpose, and with a willingness to step into one's light and power. I offer private mentorships in my 3-months signature container Divine Emerging, online group programs and international transformative retreats.

It is my heartfelt belief that we are all here to live our most outrageously awe-inspiring life and that we all hold sacred codes and medicine to share with the world. When we allow ourselves to unleash from illusionary boundaries, we are ready to serve the greater whole, create immense impact within our families, communities and the world at large, and become the earth custodians and keepers of Light we decided to be in this lifetime and beyond. It is when we assume full responsibility for our Soul's journey and are honoring all of life; and most of all, the Divinity and infinite potential we have all been gifted with. We have a responsibility in the massive shift of the Collective and we have chosen to be part of this linearity. To stand in truth and offer your part to co-create the New Earth frequency is not only an honor, it is a responsibility, and we must take it seriously. Not assuming this responsibility is not only a disservice to yourself but a disservice to all those who seek your support and sacred medicine.

In all I do, I try to see the broader picture and how, through me activating someone into their Highest timeline, I leave a ripple effect so that others too will benefit. One of my missions in this lifetime is to protect and preserve ancestral heritage of indigenous communities around the globe. Living the location-independent life that I lead, I can feel my mission unfolding in the most beautiful and unexpected ways.

I invite you to pull the ripcord and write your own story. Break the rules and forge your own true path. When you free yourself, you are one with all and you get to realize that you are a fractal of Divine Consciousness where nothing and no one can hold you back from living your Sacred Dream. All it takes is choosing and saying YES to life.

Be Fierce
Be FREE
BE YOU

ABOUT THE AUTHOR

STEPHANIE C KOEHLER

Stephanie C Koehler is the founder of StephCharlotte.com and helps visionary female entrepreneurs to create the impact they desire on their own true path.

Stephanie is an Alchemist and Accelerator of Human Potential using rituals, Quantum Healing, coaching, and shamanic practices.

She is passionate about helping others to find their voice, shift from fear to fierce turning obstacles into opportunities, and break through blockages in order to fully embody their gifts and live their Soul's purpose.

She offers private 1:1 mentorship and healings, online programs, and global transformational retreats. Stephanie loves weaving Quantum science with ancient wisdom traditions.

One of her missions is to protect the ancestral heritage of communities around the globe and help preserve these traditions for the benefit of future generations.

Location independent since June 2018, she is chasing her dream to experience 150 countries before she turns 90—currently Mexico!

Website: www.stephcharlotte.com
Instagram: https://www.instagram.com/stephckoehler

Facebook: https://www.facebook.com/stephanie.koehler.1466
Facebook: https://www.facebook.com/groups/AlchemyHub/
Email: steph@stephcharlotte.com

22

TATIANNA MICHALAK

THE HARMONY OF SUCCESS

*H*ello beautiful soul!

Firstly, I would love to say, thank you for diving into this chapter with me. My intention for you as you read along is that you feel empowered, illuminated, and open minded.

If you were to Google the 'definition of success', you would most likely find an answer along the lines of 'the accomplishment of a purpose'. I believe that 'success' wears many different hats; and it is actually quite different from what society has taught us. The amount of money in the bank, driving an expensive name-brand car, and owning a mansion or a yacht do not define success. These are merely the materialistic aspect of it. Success is pictured differently depending on who you ask, but it is most important to remember that your idea of success should be unique to you. By the end of this chapter, we will come to know that you have all of the necessary "ingredients" inside of you to become YOUR idea of success.

In 2019, I discovered the art of sound healing and in the year that followed I became a certified sound healer. Since then, I have worked with many different types of souls. If you aren't familiar with sound healing, it has been around for thousands of years, dating back to ancient Greece when it was used to cure mental disorders. Instruments such as the didgeridoo have been used by the indigenous Australians as well as the Himalayan (or Tibetan) singing bowl some 40,000 years ago for healing ceremonies. Vocal chants were also used to ward off evil spirits in some cultures. Some of these approaches have been forgotten, but within the last twenty years, sound healing has become more popular within the Western society for the practices that remain. As a certified sound healer, I use healing instruments such as crystal alchemy sound bowls, tuning forks, as well as my clients' voice to tap into their own unique sound. When you are able to raise your internal vibration, your desires will begin to manifest into the physical world.

Sound healing wasn't always a part of my life. In 2017, I was diagnosed with anxiety and depression after a toxic relationship had left me spiraling. Anxiety and panic attacks happened on a weekly if not daily basis, and I just couldn't seem to figure out what was causing them. Looking back at that particular time in my life, to others my life seemed picture-perfect. I had so many amazing things going on: I graduated with a bachelor's degree from Quinnipiac University in Diagnostic Imaging; I had secured a great job as a sonographer fresh out of college at a hospital; just bought a new car; was surrounded by great family and friends. But I still felt empty inside. I was literally living the life that so many people would consider to be "successful", but in reality I felt nothing of the sort. I was numb. There was no antidepressant or anti-anxiety medication in the world that made me feel like me. I had hit rock bottom and felt as if I was drowning there. If you don't believe the world works in mysterious ways, I can attest that it truly does. I believe that everything happens for a reason and if this wasn't a sign from above, then I don't know what else to call it!

One day, I happened to come across a woman online named Susy Schieffelin. She was offering a "sound bath". I had never heard of it before, but I was intrigued. I had to research. The only bath I was familiar with was the one you take in the comfort of your home, or on vacation in a nice hotel. I don't know exactly what led me to sign up for Susy's virtual sound bath, but it just felt right. It was an experience I will never forget. She was surrounded by sound bowls and had me lay down and closed my eyes. As soon as Susy began to play, sound washed over every fiber of my being. My thoughts no longer were racing, and peace overcame me. This was the first time I had ever experienced the harmonics of the sound bowls. My body and mind were in this beautiful, spiritual state of ease. Suddenly, the unbearable weight I had been subconsciously holding onto had lifted. I was completely in tune with my body. The sound of my mind connecting to a higher power completely drowned out any surrounding noises. It was the most alive I have ever felt, with no medication involved. It was at this exact moment that I realized I needed to delve deeper into the world of sound. Unfortunately, Susy lived in California and I was here in Connecticut. Ironically, at the time I was reading "The Alchemist" by Paulo Coelho. It's about a young boy who follows his heart's desires, pursues his dreams unapologetically, and everything aligns and falls into place. One of my favorite quotes from the story is on page 22: "And, when you want something, all the universe conspires in helping you to achieve it."

Susy announced she was doing an East Coast sound bowl tour. To my surprise, she only had three dates, all which were located in Connecticut. Was this a coincidence, or was it the universe conspiring to help me?

With the guidance of Susy Schieffelin and Jeralyn Glass, I trained with crystal alchemy bowls, chimes, and healing voices in the beautiful Santa Barbara, California. My biggest takeaway from my training was, and always will be, *sound*. Whether it is from our own vessel, or from a sacred healing instrument, it can shift frequencies from lower energies such as fear, guilt, and shame, and help raise the vibrations to include love and joy. I also learned of the power of intention, positive thought and speech and their ability to truly heal lives and shape the outside world around us. Where our intention goes, our energy flows. Jeralyn further explained that each chakra in the body has its own vocal tone, and when said out loud or chanted, it can work through certain blockages over time and allow emotional releases. When vibrations travel through the body, it travels mostly through the water that makes up 65% of us. Water is an incredible conductor of sound. As it travels, the body will hear it and recognize its own distortion and autotune itself into harmony. If you are not familiar with Dr. Massaru Emoto, he is famously known for his work involving speaking words into water and seeing how the vibration of a particular word affects the water. Phrases such as "I can't" or "I hate you" have such negative and low vibrations, that if you speak it into a bottle of water and study it under a microscope, it will be in a rather ugly formation. Incredibly, that same water changes completely when phrases such as "I love you" are said. The positive and high vibrations are then turned into a water crystal that is beautiful and symmetrical. Our bodies long to be spoken to in harmonious words.

During my journey with sound, I discovered my voice and began to integrate it into my body. This is a constant work of art and meaning, and I work on this every single day. The voice is our own personal instrument of healing, yet so many of us lose sight of it. Almost every known religion started off with some sort of deity speaking life into existence. We live in the uniVERSE – a verse is a part of a song. Indigenous American shamans tell a story that says the heart was the first drum. That is why we call it a "heartbeat". Sound is interwoven into many creations of the world; all we have to do is tune in and listen. When we sing, we tell stories with our words. From a scientific standpoint, there is a nerve in our bodies called the "vagus nerve". It connects all of the major organs through one cranial nerve. When an individual uses their voice, the vagus nerve responds to the sound, and provides a direct line of communication to the major organ systems. This enables balance between both hemispheres of the brain, creating a harmony of the mind and body.

We are electrical and vibrational beings. When a house is supplied with electricity, there must be a grounding wire that connects and grounds to the earth. The earth has a natural heartbeat of about 7.8 hertz. Meawhile, a cat's purr resonates at around 25 hertz; at this same exact frequency, bone growth, tissue regeneration, and fracture healing occur. When we are in nature, while tuning into the earth with our bare feet, we naturally relax and heal. It is much harder to tune into the natural rhythm of the earth in a space like New York City full of man-made noise. All of this "pollution" has caused a rise in distress and imbalance within the circadian rhythm and our peace.

2020 was a hell of a year, to say the least. For me, I found myself working on the front lines during the COVID-19 pandemic, about thirty minutes outside of New York City, the U.S. epicenter. Never in my life have I ever experienced something as ugly as this virus. Never in my life had I seen so many sick people, fighting for their lives. As a licensed sonographer, my job consisted of scanning for blood clots in positive-infected patients. I struggled with bridging the gap of not being able to speak to ventilated patients. I love speaking positively with my patients and guiding them calmly through my scans. While doing more research regarding healing, I stumbled upon Rebecca Llewellyn, a shamanic breathwork practitioner. She incorporates many indigenous American roots into her work. Her work taught me that, instead of fearing my workplace and job, I should instead turn it into something that is sacred. Every day should be lived in gratitude and harmony. Although this unpredictable and terrifying virus left me in so much fear and low-vibrating emotions, I was able to give my hands, my personal vessel, as an instrument for healing. When you are healed, you are able to give yourself to the universe and help others heal. The most important thing to learn is to trust in the universe. It will always take care of you. When you radiate positive energy and intention, it spreads.

Currently, I work at an OB/GYN office. I make it a point to start everyday with positive affirmations and the intention to create a healthy and healing environment that will allow my patients to feel safe and at ease. I also play sound bowl frequencies on my laptop for my patients; they adore it!. It sets the tone of the room without consciously realizing it. Outside of my day job, I work with clients as a healer one-on-one and in group settings. I work with all kinds of people, from those who suffer from debilitating anxiety and panic attacks to cancer patients to help them turn off the outside noise and tune into their soul frequency. There, the body starts to align and the healing begins resulting in an unexplainable balance. When there is a disease in the body, it means that there is an area of dis-ease. There is a blockage causing disharmony and imbalance. Our bodies naturally crave harmony.

Healing is not complicated, and it certainly doesn't have to consist of medication. But the most crucial element is for the client to maintain a positive outlook and truly believe they will heal. Open mindedness can truly work wonders.

When I first looked at success, it was something that I wanted to achieve. But it also had very negative associations like greed, corruption, and anger. It seemed the more riches you have, the more powerful you are. But we know riches do not define success. It is a materialistic benefit. The unrealistic expectations and standards of today's society are suspect. Success has been distorted by society; they would have us believe that it is outside of ourselves. The world doesn't need any more greedy, powerful or "successful" people. What the planet needs is healers , peacemakers, and heart-centered actions from souls that pursue harmony and unity in this world. Before I discovered sound, I was unsure of where I fit in. I now realize that I want no part in whatever "normal" is considered to be, and would rather be at eternal peace within myself and everything around me. I was determined to change my thoughts around success for myself and my clients. Feeling inferior is a mindset. It divides us. Yet positive intention and prayer can turn darkness to light.

Success to me is being in a harmonious state. Growing up, I thought that being successful meant you had something to prove to others, or something that was achieved after years of working hard. But over time, I finally started to realize that success is actually a mindset and something we can tap into in every present moment. I have reached my own success because I have been able to pursue my passion while staying in harmony within myself and those around me. Success should never compromise your integrity or values. It should never make you change who you are as a person to accomplish it. Success is not defined by today's societal "norms". It is instead a constant work of art. Your success journey may not look the same as mine, or as your family and friends – but do not let that discourage you from staying on your particular path. Your soul frequency will guide you where you want to go, but more so, where you *need* to go in order to live in true happiness.

Always remember that your journey will not be perfect. There will be challenges along the way that try to throw you off balance, but it is important that you realize these obstacles are only tests. They will push you to your limits, but you will conquer the fear. Use your tools to help you along the way, such as sound healing. Since bringing sound into my life, I have experienced true miracles. I have been able to work through the ebbs and flow of life much more gracefully. I have also noticed that people or situations that consist of low vibrations and bad energy will no longer affect my happiness. I encourage you all to move through your life by singing your own unique song; it's yours for the taking. Continue to seek your own true frequency. The positive vibrations that we put out into the world cannot be silenced. We must always rise above.

The truth of the matter is we do not have all the answers. I can't tell you which way is the "right" way, but I can tell you that you will find your "right" way. I encourage you to use the methods I have provided you with and just go for it. Take the leap. Raising your frequency can change your life, improve over health and mental health, as well as your general wellbeing. Please, take a few minutes for yourself daily. Take off your socks and shoes, place your feet on the ground, close your eyes, and tune into the earth's natural rhythm; magic will happen. When you are able to silence all of the background noise and radiate your positive energy into the earth, it will come back tenfold.

Always follow your dreams and place positive intentions and thoughts into all you do. The ripples and waves of energy and sound will carry you to amazing places.

Please allow me to thank you all for taking the time to read my chapter. I am truly enlightened to share my experiences and knowledge of sound and success with you. I would also like to give gratitude to everyone that has not only believed in me, but supported me throughout my own success journey. To my mother: Mom, thank you for giving me the best foundation to grow as an individual, and for always encouraging me to use my voice. To my father: Dad, thank you for always teaching me the power of positivity and happiness. You are my inspiration, I truly am you. To my amazing boyfriend G, and our pup, Gretzky, you two are my world. Thank you for always being patient and loving me unconditionally. Susy and Jeralyn, you have truly taken me under your wings and have opened my heart up to sound. Khem, thank you for further encouraging me to use my voice – it is a powerful tool. Rebecca, thank you for teaching me the power of gratitude and prayer. Robin, thank you for your love and safety. To the rest of my family and friends, I love you, I appreciate you, and I am sending positive energy and vibrations your way. Where we go one, we go all.

ABOUT THE AUTHOR

TATIANNA MARIA MICHALAK

Tatianna Maria Michalak is a trained sound and Sekhem energy healer based in Shelton, Connecticut. She has studied sound and energy healing under Jeralyn Glass, Khem Reyall, and Susy Schieffelin. She believes that her purpose on earth is to assist her clients by teaching them how to raise their frequencies with the use of Crystal Alchemy sound bowls and tuning forks. Her gift of healing guides her clients to enter a sacred place within, allowing them to unearth the unique sound of their soul. She dedicates her work to expanding the use of music, sound, and voice as therapeutic and transformational modalities. She hopes to inspire the world to embrace music as a catalyst for healing.

Tatianna graduated from Quinnipiac University in 2015 with a bachelor's degree in Diagnostic Imaging. She lives life surrounded by sound and enjoys spending time with her family, her boyfriend Garrett, their puppy Gretzky, and fluffy cat Mama.

Website: https://www.wavesofharmonyhealing.com/
Instagram: https://www.instagram.com/waves_of_harmony
Email: tatianna.michalak@gmail.com

23

EXALTED PUBLISHING HOUSE

*B*ridget Aileen Sicsko is the founder of Exalted Publishing House, a Podcast Host and Leadership Consultant. She helps successful entrepreneurs standout and be featured as a leader in their industry through sharing powerful stories, writing best-selling books and gaining global recognition. Bridget also hosts a Podcast called "The Gathering MVMT" where she has interviewed over 60 entrepreneurs, TedX speakers, authors, thought-leaders, & visionaries to discuss the realms of unlimited potentiality, kundalini yoga, metaphysics, energetics and quantum reality. Bridget has been featured in Authority Magazine, Thrive Global, The Medium, on Ticker News, News 12 New York and numerous podcasts. She lives in New Jersey with her husband and border collie - beagle, Finn.

Bridget's hope behind these books is to bring information, knowledge, wisdom and hope to people all over the world. She believes in the power of words, stories and voices to shift the way we view reality, our potential and our purpose on the planet.

Website: www.bridgetaileen.com
Email: bridget@bridgetaileen.com
Facebook Community: www.facebook.com/groups/rockthemiconline
Instagram: www.instagram.com/blissfulbridget
Podcast: https://podcasts.apple.com/us/podcast/the-gathering-mvmt/id1546684870

Manufactured by Amazon.ca
Bolton, ON